Creativity

Creativity

JD Roman
Manuel Ferrández

libros
en red

www.librosenred.com

C.E.O.: Marcelo Perazolo
Cover Design: Daniela Ferrán
Cover Photo: Manuel Ferrández
Interior Design: Juan Pablo Vittori

Design, typesetting, and other prepress work by LibrosEnRed
www.librosenred.com

ISBN: 978-1-59754-670-6

© LibrosEnRed, 2011

Prologue

Frogs are amphibians that adapt their body temperature to their surrounding environment. If we grab a frog and drop her into a pot filled with cold tap water - you can use mineral water, that doesn't disrupt the process - and then we put the above-mentioned container on the kitchen stove (with the frog still inside) and then we start heating the water, we will be the witnesses to a very curious and, at the same time, utterly didactic phenomenon.

The water starts heating up slowly but steadily. The frog, nevertheless, adjusts her body temperature to the environment, not encountering, at first, any problem to do it. The water though, inexorably, continues warming up. And the frog, again, is capable of adapting the temperature of her body, now with some more effort and using more energy than previously, truth to be said. The water continues warming up… and do you surmise how this whole fascinating pedagogic process ends up? Yes, you have won: eventually we've got some nice frog stew.

It is true that our frog can adapt her body temperature to her environment, but, logically, only to some extent. From there on, her life is literally in peril. So why doesn't she jump out of the pot in which she is immersed? Simply because she has the conviction - evidently erroneous - that this time, as usual, she still will be able to self-adapt. Why, she has done it in other many occasions in the past and, in all of them, most successfully.

Unfortunately, this syndrome, which we might call the "cooked frog syndrome", affects many organizations, companies, teams and people. In the daily reality in which we are immersed, there have been many people who were fully convinced of the fact that they could adapt to the always changing surrounding environment, when, suddenly, they have realized that change was much more drastic than they had imagined at first. Lamentably, in no few occasions, the outcome is predictable and inevitable: they end up turning themselves into some "cooked frogs".

We don't think we are committing any outrage on common sense if we affirm that if we always do the same thing, we are always going to obtain the same results (beside assuming that all of the already existing parameters remain the same, otherwise the results could actually be even worse).

In a global and increasingly competitive world, the aptitude to generate and manage new ideas that may turn into valuable projects or innovations has become a competitive edge indispensable for the survival of the organizations, for the professionals who live in them and for all those people with entrepreneurial spirit. In other words, the capacity of adjustment to new situations turns out to be vital.

This capacity for adjusting to the surrounding environment can be analyzed from two directions. One of them is clearly reactive. It takes place when, having perceived the changes in our surroundings, we decide that we won't be able to sustain our current level of results. The attempt at adjustment is then triggered because of a new existing situation.

The second strategy, on the other hand, is proactive. In this case, it is about anticipating the tentative oncoming changes.

Obviously, the latter approach implies many risks, but, in the majority of cases, it turns out to be much more effective. The first approach, the reactive one, though often successful and achieving the proper adjustment to the new circumstances, may fail: the response comes too late (not to speak about the amount of time and energy that it requires).

Actually, we don't have an exact idea of what is going to happen in the future and, therefore, of how the changes will unfold. Nevertheless, we are sure of this: the skill that will help us the most when confronting changes and crisis with acceptable guarantees of success is creativity.

But, what do we exactly mean when we mention the word creativity? Is it something magic? Is it a gift some people are blessed with and some others not?

Unfortunately, the so-called "epistemic dualism", quite present in some other fields, looms over the concept of creativity. It is a classic debate, initiated in times of the ancient Greeks, about whether such a skill is innate or acquired (in other words, the endless debates between the influence of heredity *versus* the influence of education; nature *versus* nurture).

We, personally, do contemplate creativity in the same way as any other skill; and definitely not as something magic that some people possess and some others don't. We think that, as it happens with many other skills, we will find a negligible minority of human beings who are "naturally creative" and a crushing majority that is not naturally creative.

So, to some extent, creativity can be learnt. Whatever our level of innate talent, anybody can develop his creativity, thru study and, especially, thru practice.

Consistent with this belief, in this book we approach creativity as being just a skill that, we are pretty sure of, it is possible to nurture and develop.

Once you agree with that this affirmation is legit and acceptable, there's another series of questions that comes to our mind: what makes possible that some people are more creative than others? Or the fact that specific individuals are more creative in some concrete circumstances and not in others? How is it possible to develop creativity in an effective form? What results can be expected after having developed the above-mentioned skill? Do some tricks and techniques exist that enable us work on creativity?

This book brings forward some answers to all of those questions. And it tries to do it in a clear and positive way. From our perspective as trainers and coaches, we are sure that, for any people and for any organization, it turns out to be fundamental to promote and heighten the creativity skill as a tool for personal and professional development.

The structure we have adopted for the present book has appeared quite obvious to us. We have deemed suitable to start by addressing some general questions about creativity as what it is exactly, what are the different aspects that determine and influence it, and the skills (or "muscles") that it is necessary to workout. In the second part, we have focused on creativity in a managerial environment.

Then, we have dedicated a section of the book to presenting the origin and, especially, the utilization of some of the most relevant creative techniques that we have used in our trainings in-company. In the final part, we include two sections that focus eminently on practice. In the section called *"Creative challenges"* we invite the readers to tease their brains thru some exercises and problems that, in order to be solved, need to put in gear our creative muscles. The readers can use that section to unlock the mind and to stimulate their creativity.

Finally, we present a series of ideas to develop your creativity on a daily basis. That section gets the name of *"Personal Action Plan"* and we assure that, if you cling to all the advices and suggestions herein exposed, you will notice how your creativity starts soaring.

Actually, each of the different sections can be read in an independent form. We are sure, nevertheless, that if the reader sticks to the progression we propose, it will turn out to be easier to understand the foundations, the essence and the why of the techniques for creativity development.

So be prepared for this trip that is on the verge of setting forward. And bear in mind the following phrase, as it will be very useful to help you approach this book and, also, why not say it, to develop your creativity:

> "Mind is like a parachute,
> It works only when it is opened".

1

THE FOUNDATIONS OF CREATIVITY

The word creativity has its origin in the Latin term *create*, that means to generate, to produce, and to create. According to this etymology, creativity is a dynamical activity, an open session that also leads to a material and concrete accomplishment.

For many centuries it has been thought that creativity was a divine gift and that a few chosen creative people exist (the geniuses!) and that there is a huge crowd of people who are not creative. Today it is demonstrated that this is not true. Every human being is creative... although many people do not know it yet. But as there are as many definitions of creativity as there are specialists, in this book we suggest the following one: *it is the art of perceiving problems and proposing solutions.*

Just like any form of art, creativity has some – unlimited - techniques that allow us stimulate the imagination and apply it to the resolution of different problems that affect a company, a team or a single person.

In fact, the equation of creativity can be represented in the following form:

A + B = C

"A" is a problem or a concern

"B" is an image, something that we perceive, and which may not be related to our problem..

"C" is the idea that blossoms when we link our problem "A" to the image "B".

(Now I look at this ashtray, I know how to fix my parking problem!).

Let's remember, using that formula, some universally known examples:

Newton had a problem "A": "Why do planets travel around the Sun instead of roaming free through the outer space?". One day he got the image "B": The apple that falls down the tree. After associating his problem "A" with the image "B" (a small ball, an apple, attracted by a big ball, the Earth) arose the idea "C": The law of universal gravitation.

About Archimedes, well, he was facing a curious challenge "A": calculate the exact volume of a chiseled wreath. The image "B" came after contemplating the elevation of the water level once he stepped into his tub. Once having associated "A" and "B" arose (Eureka!) the idea "C": Archimedes's principle.

The problem "A" of Gutenberg was of a somewhat more spiritual nature: he wanted to spread the Bible so the whole world could read it. The image "B" he perceived was double: on one hand, the stamps that were used for sealing letters and, on the other one, the wine presses. The union of "A" and "B" is what today allows our readers hold this very book in their hands.

How would the world look like if Newton had not rested in the shade of a tree, if Archimedes had not had the healthy habit of bathing, if Gutenberg was agnostic (no "A") or had never stumbled over a press (no "B"), if Fleming had not pored over a Petri box he had forgotten to wash or if Bell had not felt curiosity for the bones in our internal ear? Evidently, we cannot know. But, undoubtedly, without those ideas and inventions the world would be something very different from what we know today.

During the last years a series of techniques have been developed, which, on one hand, allow us define clearly the problems "A" and, on another one, help us stimulate the emergence of images "B". As we will see, many of these techniques base their methodology on consciously provoking this emergence (instead of solely hoping that mere luck will link the problem with the image). This set of techniques leads to creativity (seen as a process) or, in a more sophisticated expression, to heuristic.

In general, creativity and innovation are understood as practically synonymous concepts and although they are actually intimately related, they are not, as we will see, exactly the same thing.

Creativity constitutes a help for the solution of problems inside an organization. As we say, it gives us new tools for analyzing the nature of a problem and for generating a wide variety of options for its solution.

On the other hand, the concept of innovation represents in itself, a creative solution; i.e. it supposes a change realized with the intention of solving a problem or of improving an existing situation.

So we might define both terms the following way:

- **Creativity** is the mental process that helps us generate ideas.
- **Innovation** is the practical application of those ideas within an effective organization.

As we see, both concepts are related because, in an organization, creativity only has some meaning when its practical application is pursued, namely innovation.

Characteristics of creativity

It is a confirmed fact that some people are very creative, when on the other hand, some are quite conservative. An analysis of the characteristics of the brain can help us clarify the dynamics of creativity and the reason of the existence of different degrees of creativity in different people.

There are many authors who coincide in defining the factors or essential characteristics of creativity as being:

Fluency

It is the facility to generate a high number of ideas. This capacity appears clearly when people, before some tasks, must produce great quantity of answers in a given time.[1] It is likely that the more ideas we bring forward when we have to solve a problem, the better results will be achieved. Quantity, in the end, is the mother of quality. Numerous studies certify it. Quality will come later.

---

1   The best ideas tend to appear quite late in the process, whatever we are in a meeting or working on an ideas generation process. Actually, it has been analyzed that the last 50 ideas are of much better quality than the first 50 ones. When we split the duration of the session into two equal length parts, we see that during the second half, 80% of good quality ideas are generated (i.e. useful ideas, and besides quite uncommon ones).

FLEXIBILITY

Flexibility is a characteristic of creativity by means of which the process self transforms to reach the solution of the problem. It proceeds from the aptitude to approach the problems from different angles.

The way we see it, it is confirmed that creativity has more possibilities of emerging when people walks a new path, switches their point of view for a new one, eventually spontaneously changes the method of raising a problem.

Because of it, creative people use to be people that accept with facility the point of view of others, allowing thus that only the most suitable criterion should prevail when confronting a certain problem.

ORIGINALITY

The creative thinker produces new ideas, i.e. original. Originality is then a characteristic of creativity that refers to the idea, to the process or to the product, as something new or different. We talk here about the production of ingenious or infrequent answers. Originality implies separating ourselves from the obvious, from the common places, breaking the routine by means of thinking.

The original ideas are, statistically, infrequent. Normally, they are described as unique, surprising, "mad", unusual, anti-conventional, new, mysterious or revolutionary.

It is evident that certain courage is needed in order to be creative, because every time somebody proposes a new idea, that somebody is looked upon, deemed "to be weird", in other words, belongs to a minority. And belonging to a minority is never very comfortable. For that reason, the original thinker must be prepared to confront scorn and skepticism, what his ideas will probably face. Later we will return to this point once we have reviewed the most habitual creative blockades.

There are three ways of measuring originality: rarity, distance and quality.

Rarity is easy to gauge. It is possible to observe the frequency of a response in a test conducted with a certain number of people. The creative or original ideas are the ideas that only have been presented once (or none, if the criteria we use are more rigorous).

Distance refers to the problems where it is about finding a third word related to two distant concepts. For example, the words "tree" and "bread" to be associated with the word "bark".

Finally, quality, as we had said, should be a by-product of quantity.

VIABILITY

Aptitude to produce ideas and solutions that are practically realizable.

PRODUCTION

It is the level of detail, development or complexity of the creative ideas.

The first three enunciated factors - fluency, flexibility and originality - are functions of the so-called divergent or lateral thinking, which acts as an explorer. As we will see, it is about a kind of thinking that is not paralyzed before a problem; it is the kind of thinking that realizes free association of ideas and images. It is the one that appeals to the restructuration of reality in a new way. Definitively, the one that triggers creativity.

On the contrary, convergent thinking evokes ideas and tries to link them to an already existing and well-defined point, although, at that moment, the latter remains unknown to the people involved in the process.

"CHEATING" THE BRAIN

As we have mentioned, a creative person is the one that processes in new ways the information she has, and the sensory information that we all receive. And any people can do this.

They are many experts who have recognized certain differences in the processes of gathering information and transforming it creatively. The recent discoveries about cerebral functions splash many light on these processes. We talk about a dual process.

The human brain, seen from above, has the aspect of a walnut. It presents two rounded forms, with a convoluted surface, and connected by their centers. Each of these two halves receives the name of "hemisphere".

The nervous human system is connected to the brain by a crossed connection, i.e. that the right hemisphere controls the left side of the body and the left hemisphere controls the right side. The most visible external effect of this functional asymmetry is the predominance in the use of one hand - usually the right - on the other one - the left -.

For quite a long time, scientists have known that the function of language and its related capacities are located in the left hemisphere. Language and talk are narrowly connected through the reasoned thinking function and through other superior functions, at least in relation to other animals. Maybe for this reason did the scientists think that the left hemisphere was the most important part of the brain, the domineering part, whereas the right hemisphere was the subordinate. This drove to an underestimation of the enormous potentials of the right hemisphere.

Later on, the investigations provided new information and forced the scientists to rethink their opinion in relation to the capacities of both halves of the brain.

That way, the investigations and discoveries of Roger Sperry and its collaborators (deserving the Nobel prize in 1983) on the functions of the cerebral hemispheres supposed a real revolution.

As a result of their investigations, we know now that each hemisphere is specialized in different functions. The left, the domineering hemisphere in the majority of people, is specialized in functions related to the verbal part, to the capacity of analysis, in carrying out logical reasoning, abstractions, in solving numerical problems, in learning theoretical information, in realizing deductions...

On the other hand, the right hemisphere is specialized in functions related to perception or spatial orientation, to emotional behavior (with the faculty to express and perceive emotions), and with the faculty to control the non verbal aspects of communication, with intuition, with recognition and with recollection of faces, voices and melodies. The right brain thinks and records in images.

The right hemisphere, actually, is the one that connects more directly with the creative processes.

In fact, many of the creative techniques have their essence in the attempt of "cheating the brain"; this is, in "disconnecting" the left hemisphere and activating the right one. How?

Essentially, presenting the brain a task that the left hemisphere cannot fulfill.

We attribute to very creative people, people like Leonardo Da Vinci, the double capacity, both of closely analyzing logical sequences, and of having a considerable imagination and power of synthesis. The so-called geniuses, in fact, combine their linguistic, numerical and analytical aptitude with their imagination in order to produce most of their creations. In those people, both hemispheres are deeply interconnected.

But, as we said, such a process is within reach of anyone, at least to some extent. It is not necessary to create a dilemma in the utilization of both hemispheres. Actually, in spite of the fact that both in our daily language and in our collective thinking abound the words and expressions where it appears that the right hand (and therefore the left hemisphere) is the good thing, the just thing, the moral thing, etc., actually real contraposition does not exist between the right and the left hemisphere.

Contraposition does not exist between logical thinking and creative thinking. In the same way that are not valid the divisions between thinking and feeling, between reason and intuition, between objective vision and subjective vision either.

More concretely, the efficiency of logical thinking can be promoted by means of the utilization of creative thinking techniques that, as we were saying, are orientated towards reducing the inflexibility and the automatic flow of logical thinking.

What's more, a creative solution has to be retrospectively logical; it must fit in a logical way in all the pieces of the "puzzle" that constitute the problem. A creative solution, to be valid and of some interest, must provide a better solution to the problem we want to be solved, than the one that is obtained by means of the application of the already known processes.

Definitively both types of thinking are necessary and totally complementary. They just process information in a different way.

Characteristics of the cerebral hemispheres	
LEFT	RIGHT
Verbal	**Thinks with images**
Uses words to name, to describe, to define	Has a minimal relation with the words.
Analytical	**Synthetic**
Solves the problems step by step	Groups things to form a set
Symbolic	**Concrete**
Uses symbols for representing things	Relates to things as they are in the present time
Abstract	**Analogical**
Takes some small piece of information and uses it to represent the whole set	Sees similarity between things, understands the metaphorical relations
Time oriented	**Unaware of time**
Bears the time in mind. Arranges things in succession one after another	Has no sense of time
Rational	**Needs neither the reason nor the information.** Postpones its judgments.
Extracts conclusions being based on the reason	
Digital	**Spatial**
Uses numbers	Sees the relations between things and the way in which the parts join to form a set
Logical	**Intuitive**
Extracts conclusions based on logic. One thing follows the other in a logical order	Performs leaps in comprehension based on incomplete information, hunches, sensations or visual images.
Lineal	**Holistic**
Thinks in terms of linked ideas, one thing after the other.	Sees the totality of the things at once. Perceives the forms and the structures in their entirety.

How does our mind function?

The mind works as an optimizing system for the treatment of information, as a self-organizing system. For it, it forms and uses frames and models, to avoid chaos. At the same time, it is very efficient as it allows us save energy and avoids us the need to always think in a conscious and premeditated way. For that reason, the mind creates mental routines.

The so-called "vertical" thinking, as opposed to the creative or "lateral" thinking, works with etiquettes, handling archetypal sets of information.

It works selecting, rejecting and combining known models. It polarizes, names, removes, and organizes.

It possesses a fundamentally verbal and cultural component. It creates codes and guidelines that, sometimes, get confused with reality, as by definition models are an explanation of reality, of facts, not of reality itself.

The "vertical" thinking serves to fathom into a certain direction (digging into a single hole), not drilling new holes (where probably we could find some fresh water).

The best advantage of "vertical" thinking (its permanent character) is also its principal disadvantage as it yields inertia and inflexibility. Also it is binary, not taking advantage of the possible positive contents of an alternative formula. It is just like people who at the moment of emitting their vote in a political election have to decide between political opposite formations, without being able to pick positive elements from both programs.

Thanks to the investigations led by some behaviorist psychologists we now know that the above explanation fits quite nicely with part of the psychic reality. The repetitive acts and the behavioral habits both create inside our brain some probabilistic paths that produce automatic behaviors from which it is not easy to escape.

Definitively, vertical (or logical thinking) is the type of thinking we tend to use most of the time and it works as a concatenation of correct ideas step by step.

LATERAL THINKING

The term "lateral thinking" was coined by the Maltese psychologist and physiologist Edward de Bono as a contraposition and complement to the already known vertical or logical thinking.

The fundamental purpose of this thinking style is the paradigm shift. It is both an attitude and a way of processing information. Actually, it is a set of processes aimed at the utilization of the new information so the latter can generate creative ideas by means of the restructuration of concepts already residing in the brain.

As we have seen, our mind is characterized by the creation of fixed models of concepts, which limits the possibility of utilization of some possibly new available information, unless it possesses some way to restructuring the already existing models.

And it is here where lateral thinking enters; as besides restructuring these models (its basic function), it allows us create new ones (creativity).

A good way of examining lateral thinking and understanding it more exhaustively is contemplating it in contraposition to vertical thinking:

Types of thinking	
Vertical or logical	**Lateral**
Is selective	Is creative
Only moves if there is a direction towards we can move	Can wander without any predefined direction
What imports is the logical quality of all the information	What imports is the efficiency of the results
Every step has to be correct	It is not necessary for every step to be the right one
The whole relation has a link with the problem	The sought information can have nothing to do with the problem
It is based on reason and on valuation	Discards any form of judgment or valuation
Moves forward in a sequential form	Progresses through leaps
Discards the ideas that do not have a solid base on which to rely	Doesn't reject any idea or option
Seeks quality	Seeks quantity
Follows the most evident paths	Follows all the possible paths, without excluding any of them
Is a finite process	Is a probabilistic process
The search is interrupted when satisfactory response is found	The search goes beyond the satisfactory response

As we were previously saying, there is no such thinking better than another. What we need is to develop our skills in both types of thinking. However, the prevailing educational models have always generated an exclusive worship for logical thinking. We will dedicate a few pages of this book to analyzing this tremendous paradox.

To restructure information it is necessary first to loose the preexisting rigid models. In a similar form as logical thinking uses the "NO" for the selection of alternatives, De Bono creates a new linguistic form, named PO (provocation), to try to reach this relaxation in a more effective way. We will return on this concept in the chapter dedicated to the creative techniques.

The techniques of ideas generation, which favor "lateral thinking" help us avoid inflexibilities and open new paths.[2]

---

2   Here are some creative challenges to solve. Think about how you

Laterality

Flickr is the largest photographs collection in the world.

It was created by their invertors (the Butterfield couple) when developing a complex on-line game named Game Neverending, which main characteristic was that it never ended. During the creation process, the couple launched a chatroom where people could share pictures. That was the Flickr kick-off. It is a program that allows people upload their pictures and classify them thanks to a simple tags system. Then, the rest of the Internet surfers can find them easily.

Eventually, the game was cancelled, but nowadays there are more than 100 millions pictures in Flickr.

Pondering on that, the Butterfield couple says. "If we had at first decided to create a pictures management program, maybe we would have made a lot of errors".

would face them. What's the color of felicity? What's the color of Monday?, Where is the door to December? What's the smell of color green? What's the temperature of light blue hue?

BARRIERS AND BLOCKADES
TO CREATIVITY

It is evident that when we try to put into practice and develop creativity, we meet numerous barriers. Some of them are only internal (they have to deal with our own selves) and others respond to external situations.

We all possess erroneous beliefs, barriers and impediments inside us that the investigators of those phenomena refer to them as "mental walls".

Those barriers or walls are, in fact, those that prevent the proper conceptualization of a problem and, consequently, those that strongly restrict the probability of reaching its solution.

Simberg classifies the blockades under three categories:

1 - EMOTIONAL BLOCKADES:

They are the insecurities that people may feel. Some of the most common blockades are:

- **Fear of ridicule:**
  We might also include in this category the dread of being wrong. Many people tend to anticipate possible negative commentaries, tend to imagine lack of support or even feel shame when presenting a novel idea. In other words, we are too concerned about what the others think and, when acting so, we restrict ourselves. All of those mentioned blockades constitute powerful

impediments to developing creativity. Bear in mind, for example, that the sense of ridicule is submitted to social conventions and it happens that those who manage to break those rules are the people who often are considered to be creative. Although breaking the social rules does not necessarily transmogrify you into a creative people; you may just metamorphose into a mere obnoxious lad.

- **Familiarity:**
  The excessive familiarity with the problem constitutes another source of negative interference. Although some knowledge of the environment is fundamental for solving the majority of the questions derived from the performance of a function, it stands against us when we are trying to find a new path. Actually, this one is one of the reasons that make the success of many consultants. These people are effective, not because they know more about a certain topic, but because they are capable of seeing the problem with new eyes.

- **Clinging to the first idea** that comes to us:
  Very much related to the previous blockade.

- **Thinking rigidness:**
  Disability for changing our own thinking system. For example, in many occasions we place in our mind restrictions that do not exist. I.e., we implicitly impose on us more rules than those that are really given.

- **Desire of safety and of conflicts avoidance:**
  The creative ideas can generate conflicts, be they in a small or a large scale. And this circumstance is a notable impediment to creative development. Consider for

instance what would be the reaction in your company if you were proposing a plan to obtain important savings in the processes, but that these would suppose many work habits changes for many people and that could threaten the labor stability of a certain number of people.

- **Fear** of the executives and bosses and distrust towards our companions and collaborators.

- **Obsession for rapid success** (to be in a hurry to triumph).

- **Lack of impulse** for taking forward a problem up to its full solution and to experience it. In other words, lack of inner motivation.

- **Lack of will** to start up a solution.

2 - PERCEPTION BLOCKADES:

It refers to aspects of a cognitive type. This type of blockades does not allow us grasp what the problem really is. They also refer to the fact that our prejudices drive us to present the problem in an erroneous way and, therefore, to give it inadequate solutions.

Some of the more common perception blockades are:
- We can't isolate the problem. Quite often, we get engrossed with one single aspect of the problem, hence losing the global vision of the problem.
- Blockade for obsessing with the problem: one pays little attention to everything aside the problem.

- Disability to adequately define the terms of the problem.
- Perceptive rigidness.
- It prevents us from using all of our senses for observation. It also means we use excessive filters (we see only what we want to see).
- We can't perceive remote relations.
- Connections are not established between the different elements of the problem.
- We don't investigate the obvious.
- We take things as a given. We do not question what's already known, and that prevents us from discovering other approaches.
- Difficulty for distinguishing between cause and effect.

3 - CULTURAL BLOCKADES:

They are related to our learnt core values, and they are the lost difficult to overcome. Some of the most usual are:

- The desire to adapt to a socially accepted norm.
- To be practical and economic. Expressing judgments before properly analyzing the situation
- To avoid curiosity. Thinking that being curious is impolite. Usually, it is not well seen to doubt everything.
- To give too much importance to competition instead to collaboration.
- Excessive faith and confidence in reason or in logic. This is quite common in adults, who for instance tend to repress the creative, unlogical and irrational acts of the children.
- Tendency to adopt an "absolutist" attitude (all or nothing).
- Too many knowledge on the field of the problem (or, in other occasions, too few).

- To believe that daydreaming is a waste of time.
- To have little sense of humor or to think that using it is a loss of time.
- To think that tradition is a sure value.
- To think that taboos are sacred.

In this paragraph we could include a series of blockades proceeding from the environment, such as the pressures from the conformity, the authoritarian attitude (bosses and executives that have a response for everything and who do not give importance to others' ideas). As well, ridiculing any creative attempt, overvaluation of remunerations or punishments, excessive objectivity exigency, excessive worry for success, intolerance to any playful attitude, lack of support and means to make ideas function, etc.

KILLERS AND SUICIDE SENTENCES

There are some ideas that hamper our freedom for creativity. We call them assassin sentences. Some of the most usual are *"This is impossible"*, *"We don't have enough money for that"*, *"It's not the right moment"*, etc.

Other kind of sentences contains the idea that the others are not going to pay attention to us or even not value our ideas. We call them suicide ideas. Some examples: *"I know it is stupid, but..."* *"I don't know a lot about that..."*, *"You have probably already thought about it, but ..."*.

In other words, when the killer sentences crush the others' ideas; the suicide sentences kill our own.

How to annihilate creative thinking

"This is not included in the budget".
"We have already tried that".
"If that could work, surely somebody would have already suggested it".
*"You don't understand our policy
Who's the moron that has suggested this"?*
"The manufacturing department won't accept it they'll think we are crazy".
"The clients won't accept it".
"You won't convince our Top management".
"The Unions are going to protest".
"This can't work in our kind of business".
"This will increase our costs".
"Our people won't accept it".
"I won't let a young Turk show me my job".
"This is patented".
"This is not up to our quality standard".

THE SEVERAL PHASES OF CREATIVITY

Creativity, in conceptual terms, supposes the production or conception of new and original ideas, potentially useful and relevant, whatever the area, by those people who work together in a complex social system.

Under those terms, creativity is a process within an organized scheme, which is made of a series of stages that, eventually, give birth to the creative process. This process has a set of particular features that define it.

The creative process constitutes a more or less conscious phenomenon, which true nature cannot be understood, not even by creative people.

In the development of this process, there's not always the same sequence and it may happen there are some exchanges, advances and setbacks between the different phases. We do not talk about a linear process. Inside every stage a smaller cycle can exist. So the time dedicated to each phase is not necessarily the same.

Different authors present their particular vision of what, for them, constitute the phases of this process. Obviously, notable differences exist for the names of each one of the stages, nevertheless they all coincide in indicating that the process consists, in general, of the following phases: identification of a problem (aims and related proceedings), generation of solution alternatives and selection of alternatives.

Preparation

In general, creativity sprouts when there was a prior preparation along with a deep and relevant knowledge, which precedes the creative expression. The knowledge must be useful; in the managerial world, the whole organization must have access to this knowledge, so that everybody can share it.

Preparation consists of a field analysis seeking to delimit and to establish the concrete problem, analyzing the variables present in it, observing its components, their relation with the overall set and the degree of present experiences.

The different members of an organization face, in a conscious or unconscious form, those aspects of the problem that could be interesting; therefore, the search of information constitutes a process where the people appeal both to memory and codified information and to reality. In sum, resorting to all the available sources of knowledge that help us strengthen the stage of preparation.

We must underline that this phase determines the development of other stages as, often; the best ideas use to be combinations of other ideas. Owning many materials favors the probabilities for the generation of options.

It is therefore possible to say that the preparation phase consists of "preparing the ground" for solving a problem. And it is here where it is necessary to rely on the right information to understand the context of the problem. What we claim here is that we must obtain and explore the largest quantity of possible information, and the concrete facts that are involved in the situation. This implies elaborating a strategy based in thinking about the place we currently are, in analyzing the available resources and depending on that, choosing a specific approach.

The principal objective of the definition of the territory is to obtain, with the best possible clarity, a vision of the situation (the ensuing depth will depend on the characteristics of the situation and on the available time).

Opportunity and innovation

An opportunity must exist in order to provoke creativity. This opportunity can be about improving something already existing or dealing with a threat that requires an immediate response for us to survive (before turning ourselves into cooked frogs). Often, the need for being creative proceeds from a concrete problem that has to be solved. This, on the other hand, facilitates us turning a disadvantage into a competitive edge.

In a company, the creativity process sprouts from an intention, from the sensation that something might be different, from the intention of willing to modify a currently existing situation (improve the efficiency in the meetings, reduce the traffic of electronic mail, increase sales, reduce expenses, promote teamwork between departments, etc.). All this leads us to looking for an opportunity.

The search and detection of opportunities needs us dedicate time to the thinking, to what is called "gymnastics of the thinking", a reflection that supposes an exploration without formalities, with free and open imagination. Often, nevertheless, the existence of an opportunity assumes the form of a "problem".

Divergence: Generation of options

As soon as the opportunity arises and the problem is defined, it is necessary to "design an option and put it into practice". At this stage it is imperative to overcome the different blockades, to break the restraints and apply our knowledge to reach a solution to the problem, as it is there where we will find the creative solutions.

Divergence is a new way of considering something just as if it had arisen in a sudden way, this being a moment where all the material accumulated during preparation transforms into a clear and coherent knowledge that makes possible the generation of alternatives solutions.

The generation of ideas needs fluency, flexibility and originality. Obviously, the ideas originate depending on a certain specific problem.

The creative solutions are selected from a "menu" of possibilities and we should begin with the one with the highest probability of being fruitful. The generation of options is an activity, to a certain extent, social. Because of it, the interaction with other people is fundamental.

In this stage the ideas arise in their more original form. At first glance, all the ideas possess the same value, as an idea can derive from another or from the utilization of some concrete technique or from an unexpected unforeseen relation.

Incubation

This phase relates to the necessary time to think over the identified opportunity or problem, in order to evaluate and study the diverse options generated in the stage previously described in the process. It is about a period of "standstill" where we slowly cook the problem while we devote ourselves to other questions and let our subconscious work on its own.

This phase develops then in the unconscious part of the brain. It is a time for leaning back and distancing ourselves from the analysis of the problem and the search of a solution.

The period of time that we spend without thinking directly about the problem allows us recover from the strain and, that way, be in a better disposition to centre our attention on the different elements that integrate the problem. [3]

When we stop obsessing with a problem, we make possible for the unimportant details to vanish, whereas we preserve in our memory the more relevant and significant aspects of the matter at hand. Those are actually the details that help us focus on the problem, applying another perspective and putting in play fewer limitations than the existing in our previous mental frame.

---

3   Did it never happen to you that you suddenly remember the name of a person, when a few days before you were just incapable of recalling it? We have stopped thinking of it for a while and suddenly, that name pops up in our mind without any conscious effort.

The reason dwells in our unconscious brain. The brain net connects neurons through electrical impulses in order to create thoughts. Whatever we are currently doing, neurons plow ahead with their job. That process occurs even against our own will.

And then, many ideas or solutions "unexpectedly" pop up once the unconscious finally filters organizes all the information and stimuli we have previously fed it with.

Hence, this is why it is most suitable to feed our unconscious with challenges, riddles and problems. Our unconscious brain will work on them, although we are not aware of it.

When paying attention to something different from our problem we can attenuate the belief that the approach in which we have invested a great quantity of time and energy is the best and most adapted for moving forward. Actually, that approach could be blocking the access to the desired solution.

Therefore, these pauses allow the problem to be contemplated with most clarity. We will see that many creative techniques seek this disconnection with the current situation.

The suppression of a direct implication with the problem, allows us suspend the emission of judgments, hence making possible for the problem to travel through the different states of the mind.

In the base of this process, we find the incontrovertible fact that having more time to think and to ponder redounds into a most perceptive experience (albeit unconscious).

Hence, the stage of incubation is characterized by two main features: the participation of the unconscious part of our brains and our withdrawal, at least apparently, from the problem.

At any moment, probably in the least expected one, solutions will start popping up.

CONVERGENCE: SELECTION OF OPTIONS

This stage relates to the election of an option or to a consensus about the proposed ideas. The chosen alternative must be evaluated and orchestrated and each of these activities can stimulate new opportunities.

With the application of the process we try to determine a starting point, to detect a direction for the possible alternatives, upon which we will generate the ideas and the way for moving forward. The form in which this direction is defined will be the root for the ideas that are generated later. We do not seek to solve the problem, but to elaborate an "approach" that allows us find hints to solve it.

It is a matter of deciding if the selected idea is valuable, as those tend to arise in an incomplete, untidy and confused way; therefore, the ideas must be checked and evaluated to provide them with quality and with the sufficient degree of perfection to verify their adequacy to the current problem.

As soon as the solutions have been evaluated, we start with the process of decision-making, where people will have to define and start with the solution that is the most convenient.

Once evaluated, we must ensure that the idea is novel and original.

Therefore, the ideas must be transformed into solutions, which will work only when they are useful to us. A good solution must appeal, has to convince, has to be coherent, imaginative, but simultaneously, understandably, cannot hurt too many interests; hence it must be simultaneously bold and prudent.

Besides we must determine each of the steps to continue in the application and implementation of the chosen solution in order that, later, these ideas could be put into practice, activating with it the resolution of problems. This means "in fact" to implant an innovation, where those ideas become tangible, transforming into a new product, service or process.

Inspiration / Sleeping and Dreaming

In a recent investigation, it has been discovered that students got higher marks when after having tried to solve the presented problem, they went to sleep and tried anew.

It seems that during slumber, the participants discovered some aspects they could not unveil while being awake.

The explanation is pretty simple: when we sleep, we remain active. When we sleep, our standard thinking frames weaken and our brain explores new and innovative paths and options

Slumber increases our performance and creativity, although we are not conscious of it, so when we awake, we come back with new perspectives and new ways of doing things. That's the key to incubation, and often to inspiration

---

Bed, bath, bus

Recently a survey conducted by a group of scientists fell onto our lap. They confirmed that the best, original o creative ideas are not to be found when focusing on a specific problem. On the contrary, excess in concentration tends to block our mind.

What's most useful when looking for a good idea is abstracting from the problem and just let our brain reorganize its thoughts at the unconscious level. From the areas that process that unconscious information will sprout that "Eureka" feeling.

Creative thinking connects thoughts with no apparent link between them. And our conscious brain is not able to force that process.

Hence the reason why many of our best ideas pop up in places like bed, bath or bus.

A few months ago were the 40th anniversary of the creation of the ATMs.

That brilliant idea is the offspring of a Scottish lad, who, when asked about the birthing process, told that he got that idea when enjoying a bath.

With his mind swirling with the steam, he visualized the machine as a classical vending machine, just delivering notes instead of Mars bars.

That man, John Shepherd-Barron, the inventor, states that a hot tub is a good place for thinking when we face a problem. Finally he recalls that the water was very hot.

Establishing mechanisms

We think that at this point of the book it is clear that creativity is not an over-excited act of mad inspiration, but a serious and deliberate process that can be learned.

Because of it, we should strain for establishing some mechanisms in order not to reject too rapidly the new ideas. In many occasions, those do not arise because the barriers in our own brain prevent it.

The key tools:
- Breaking the established patterns
- Applying the fundamental principles of creativity: continuity (to know how the barriers influence our minds), alternatives (how to overcome these obstacles) and provocation (to use concrete tools to break rules established in our thinking).
- Lateral thinking (as we have seen, the kind of thinking that moves freely in search of the improbable or the easily discarded).

Besides all this, we should be really convinced that being creative depends absolutely on us. We all can be creative. The setting of a series of rules and fundamental attitudes will help us in the creation process.

CREATIVE ATTITUDES

LISTEN

We listen with our ears and with all the other senses.

Hearing, for example, is our most emotionally powerful sense, more than the sight. It is the first sense that we use when in our mother's womb, as the sounds are our first contact with the exterior world. We learn to listen before being born and before seeing, or smelling or touching for the first time.

When the mother listens to a melody that produces emotions she segregate substances that affect us even in the womb, so we learn to react when hearing any external sound.

Hearing has a most associative power, empathic or suggestively that vision, taste or tact.[4]

TO LOOK (DIFFERENTLY)

The way we look at things determines what we are going to find. To be creative it is necessary to look at things the way

---

4 Thinking and drawing like a child

Many scientists have wondered up to what extent the criteria used for beholding the children's drawings are actually the point of view of an adult.

It is not just about the fact that Picasso, for instance, was a good drawer, as it is possible to train anybody in that specific skill. What's remarkable is the "spontaneity" we see in his brushstrokes, similar to a child style.

It's not about just skill; it is about the way we look at things.

children do. With an innocent look, without prejudices, without experience. An unprejudiced look. A look without corsets. A fresh look.

In order to have fresh points of view, we need fresh eyes. The habitual looks often do not allow us understand the nature of a challenge. The habit of doing, doing and doing, and solving problems, leads us to abandon - gradually but imperceptibly - the aptitude to examine things, to explore situations, to understand contexts. With this substratum, creativity is stalled.

Because of that, as we will see, seeking the help of people who know little or nothing about our field of activity in order to solve a problem is no madness. Obviously they will have to put into gear the look that's needed for being creative. The innocent look of a child.

Basically, we have to ask these people to describe what they see, to allow them ask questions and express what they do not understand and, finally, we will listen to their suggestions whenever they come up with some.[5]

As a minimum, we will obtain a series of fresh, new, different looks that will force us contemplate our problem with new eyes. With innocent eyes, just like a child.

Probably you have already heard about the method called "the pizza boy". This method uses to bring forth freshness and helps us untie new perspectives. The underlying idea is that, in many occasions, the boy who delivers the pizza can bring unimaginable perspectives to a problem or to a challenge.

---

5   **A beginner's mind**

O *nyuanshin*. In some Far East philosophy, that's the name given to a state of mind that consists of willing to walk a step back in our knowledge.

That way, we will be able to "forget" things before we start walking a new path.

Actually, it means thinking as an absolute beginner, who can see many options, whereas the expert can think only in one direction.

Why? Because he is not afraid of formulating questions, because he offers neutral observations and because his vision is simply ingenuous.

Maybe because of it, many teams that need creative approaches invite people who are not experts in the matter.

To have curiosity
Practice ingenuity and perspicacity

Chindogu and innovation

T-Shirts with incorporated fans, umbrellas with screens and Internet access, wheelchairs with GPS,... All those artifacts are part of Chindogu. That word, coined by the Japanese inventor Kenji Kawakami, means solving daily problems using gadgets.

Despite being tremendously innovative and having a practical purpose, the Chindogu artifacts end up generating more problems than solutions, or triggering such public humiliation that they are actually totally useless.

Chindogu is then full of stimulating contradictions. Being both subversive, anarchist or trivial and ingenious or plainly foolish.

Those are close words but with different meanings.

Both are the results of a certain possibility of restructuring. And in both cases the change is sudden and spontaneous.

When change has a transitory character it gives birth to ingenuity whereas when it is rather permanent it generates perspicacity.

Ingenuity is the faculty to see or invent with swiftness and facility. It has to deal with intuition, with understanding and, actually, with the creative faculties. It is also a spark or the talent to see and rapidly unveil the true nature of things.

Ingenious people can face all kinds of practical difficulty, reorganizing the surrounding world and extracting a solution, taking advantage of all the available elements at the given moment and place.

Setting up ingenuity, is like, say, being an expert in bricolage, who keeps all kind of stuff, to use them in a way totally different from the original one.

It is curious to observe that often, a keen solution provokes certain hilarity, even though the solution is not comical in itself.

Actually, in the processes of innovation the ideas that require the more attention are precisely those that provoke hilarity.

The ideas that receive immediate approval from the team are normally not the most creative ones.

Those that produce confusion can be an occasion for big advances if they are properly managed.

There are many ways of cultivating curiosity, but one of them has to do with being surprised day after day. We have the example of Chisen Chiu, a Taiwan designer. Chisen recounts how one special day, in the suburbs of Taipei, he stumbled on a factory specialized in producing recycled paper with a beehive cells structure.

Intrigued by the use of a cell structure to create sturdy board elements, he thought that that material could be used for creating any kind of rigid structure.

After a few experiments he came to an idea. With that unique material we could, for instance, make a chair. Te final product is called FlexibleLove.

It is a seat with an amazing resistance and sturdiness, especially when we realize that is made of ... paper.

So, in the end, a pile of paper garbage has been processed and transmogrified into a stretching, compactable and multi-shape seat, for one up to sixteen people.

Keeping our mind open, being curious and willing to experiment new things may lead us to creative and surprising results.

In the fifties, a famous social psychologist (Solomon Asch) conducted a series of laboratory experiments about conformism. The conclusions were adamant: we people give up when being under pressure from the group.

In many a situation, in company o in social life, when willing to solve a conflict, we apply the majority rule. Majority represents the group knowledge of the bunch, instead of the individual criteria of one single person.

The uneasiness from being alone may lead us to think that a majority opinion is more appealing than clinging to our own ideas of beliefs

USE YOUR INTUITION

Intuition is more than a hunch. Intuition is an interior perception that leads us to walk a certain path. It is like an invisible force that guides our performances.

An intuition is a rapid judgment that blossoms in our brain. The person does not know exactly why she has this sensation. Nevertheless, it is sufficiently strong to trigger a concrete behavior.

Apparently, intuitions are based often on hints that exist in the environment. When using our instinct, we are taking these hints in account and at the same time disdaining the unnecessary information.

The opposite of intuition is calculation, the rational classical approach.

Intuition, as a consequence, is a fundamental element in creativity. Often, following a certain path instead of another responds to an intuition or to a feeling. To something that cannot be explained.

Creative people are tremendously intuitive, as they possess the aptitude to reach the meaning of the deepest possibilities in an indirect form.

The experts talk about four levels of intuitive knowledge: the physical one (linked to the sensations in our body), the emotional intuition (it implies relation with another people), intuition at a mental level (the so called "intuitive flash") and the spiritual level (linked to transpersonal).

Beyond the above-mentioned classifications, it would be OK to learn how to develop the intuition and to trust in it.

Breaking the frames

It is the game of the possibilities.[6]

Vicente Huidoro, the great Chilean poet, great lover of breaking the laws of syntax, expresses it clearly in an aphorism that, to us, wonderfully illustrates this concept:

"The four cardinal points are three: North and South"

ASSOCIATE

We can realize different free associations:

- Phonetics (the same assonance of the first syllable or of the last one),
- Serial (ruff, chicory, lettuce...),
- Of proximity (flour - bread, music - violin),

---

6   **The shortest row**

Hundreds of people performing the same reckoning at the same moment: rationally analyze the length of the queues and then pick one amongst them (the one they surmise will be the quickest).

This is a "rational insanity": the more are things rationalized, the more unpredictable they become. The stock exchange or real estate market are some good examples. As there are thousands of experts analyzing every apartment, every chip, all the possible forecasts have already been analyzed, hence the unpredictability of the market (just have a look at the 2008 world-wide crisis). There is no such bargain in real estate or in stock exchange market. And of course, the shortest cash row at the supermarket doesn't exist.

What do we do then? Don't ask specialists and economists for any omen o prediction. Their forecasts are as good - or bad - as yours.

- Subjective (in reference to our own personal story),
- By opposition (black - white),
- By synonymous,
- Clichés, proverbs, ...
- Continent - content (bottle - wine),
- Changing angle (pine - coffin) or sense (church - faith).

Bi-associate

According to Koestler, biassociation is the fundamental process of creativity that consists of an instantaneous overlapping of two normally remote planes of reference. From this point of view, creativity is a consequence of a double mental process:

- **Dissociation**, which allows us get rid of our routine ways of thinking
- **Association**, which implies the creation of new relations between facts usually remote.

That's why the creative mind is the one capable of freeing himself from any acquired structure and accepting the risk of recombining and bringing together what habitually is separated.

Combine (flee from binary thinking)

Quite often, our mind contemplates things through a dual, binary lenses, yes or not, white or black, one thing or another. Nevertheless, the real world is never so binary.

In the world of materials, for example, firmness and elasticity are incompatible. Mussels, on the other hand, seem to have found the way of combining both properties. The filaments of the mussel can stretch up to 70 % without tearing apart. The scientists are close to discovering what allows their cuticles to stretch.[7]

---

7   **Thinking outside the box**

This finding might contribute to the development of bio-mimetic covers for medical implants or industrial devices. So, combining two seemingly incompatible things? Why not! Who says that it should be impossible?

BE SPONTANEOUS

Spontaneity supposes giving up, relaxing in order to increase the flow of sensations and ideas, both others' and ours.

USE YOUR BODY

We tend to think only of the mind when talking about creativity. And then we forget that we have a body, a body that determines our identity and determines our capacity of response.

There are many people who practice creativity through their body. Without going that far, we can realize a body warming before putting our brain into creative tasks.

The warm-up will activate our corporal tone and also the general functioning of the body, including - obviously - our mind.

In one of the capers of Thorgal, a comic hero created by Rosinski and Van Hamme, the hero stands before a strange artifact: a golden necklace positioned in the center of a wooden frame and tied to the four sides of the frame by 4 strings.

An ancient tradition states that the one who will, with a single arrow, free the necklace will rule the country.

The country has been kingless for many years. The thinking blockade was due to the fact that everyone associated the arrow with a bow. And obviously, it was impossible to cut four strings with a single arrow shot.

What Thorgal did was this: he took an arrow in his hand, and using it as a knife, simply cut the four strings.

Creativity has to do with thinking from other reference frames.

PLAY

Playing is an elementary function of human life. Playing is the fundamental element that allows the children develop and grow.

In order to create, we should go back to the children world, return to our infancy, to those days when imagination was our dominating impulse.

The children explore, i.e., they manipulate, open, try to thoroughly inspect everything that falls in their hands and even modify it. It is very common to observe, for example, that when a child receives a toy that works with batteries he takes it, disassemble it and with one of the parts plays cars, uses another one as a robot and the last one he uses it as a box to keep his marbles. These new functions probably will be changed into some other new functions when the child returns to explore the object, transforming the function drastically.

To explore, to experiment, to accept rules (and to change them), to check the limits ... that's the game. Playing implies having, first, the mind of a novice, of a beginner. To be open, to search, to try things, to be wrong...

Etymologically, the word comes from the chiefly word "plegian", meaning "to exercise". As a verb, "play" is defined in terms of an imaginative activity - individual or in groups - that foments discovery and game. As a noun, it refers to an activity involved in amusement or in representation.

In both senses, it is tremendously connected to the triggering of a recreative and playful mentality.

Playing, in its widest meaning, is the key to promote our aptitude to imagine and invent. As a consequence of the game, besides, amusement arises: a positive added effect that reinforces the process.

The majority of the creative techniques that we will see in the third module actually try to recreate this moment to stimulate the disconnection from the problem, to help us deal with topics that seemingly have nothing to do with it.

Any mechanism or technique that leads us to the essence of the fame is capable, therefore, of turning an idea into something potentially creative.

BOLD ATTITUDE

We take ourselves too seriously. When aging, we tend to become more rigid, prisoners of the armor we have built for protecting ourselves from the attacks from the outer world.

We stop playing, and our life becomes dull. Playing is a cure for rigidness, for routine.

Hence we must nurture boldness, adventurous attitude. We need to renew our own capacity for amazement.

ACKNOWLEDGE WITHOUT JUDGING

Agree without judging. Neither censure ourselves nor censure the others, avoid judgments. We try to produce ideas, not to evaluate them and, even less, to evaluate my power, my force or my intelligence, as inside a group the ideas belong to the group. This is what makes it productive.

When we are generating ideas in groups, speak often and briefly.

Let's see a classical situation: for the uninitiated, what's most harmful is the belief that their ideas are no good. This prevents them from developing their skills.

Actually, being a non-initiated person may hamper your capacity in some specific fields, but, on the other hand, when what is required is curiosity, thorough observation, experimentation, etc. being a profane becomes something potentially positive.

Express in a concrete way

If we speak with images, our language is alive and, thanks to it, reaches a great power of evocation in the others, offering them the possibility of building associations.

This process is totally dependent on self-control and on the respect towards the others and towards myself.

"Steal" and transform the ideas of the others

When we generate ideas in-group there is no leader. The contributed ideas are not property of anybody.

Sweat

Creative thinking is also, often, related to sweat and intensity.

Nevertheless, it is most true that thinking strenuously does not guarantee a happy result. On the other hand, it does guarantee a favorable mental set to solve the problem.

Persevere

Any innovation is based on a series of failures accumulated during a long process. Obviously, assuming that those failures have already been deeply ingrained.

People who, instead of picking tasks where they know that they can have good results pick tasks with possible failures are likely to be creative.

This is, to a great extent, the reason of their success.

Learn how to live in "disorder"

Computer programs require that the files and their icons are to be arranged in a logical form to make their location easy.

On the other, our desk uses to be a place with stacked papers, documents, reports, etc. Summarizing, a place with a certain level of chaos.

Because of that, some computer programs try to translate the habitual disorder from our tables to our digital office.

Behind their creation lies the theory of the secret benefits that disorder may yield. The predominant culture seeks cleanliness and tidiness, but eventually this turns out to be a prejudice for creativity.

STRUGGLE

Many innovations have to fight to death before they are accepted and implemented (provided that they eventually achieve it). Something as mundane as the dot on the letter "I" was accepted after a long struggle. In the 16th century, when the gothic letters were introduced, some scribes found practical to jot a dot above the "I", in order not to misread a double "I" that could be read as a "u".

Well, although it makes a lot of sense, they had to fight for years with their peers, who deemed that improvement as useless or at best plainly fussy.

GREET UNCERTAINTY

We are like that. When we believe that "we know" something, we stop paying attention. And this mechanism is very common. In the end, we are not comfortable at all with doubts and uncertainty.

To be creative, it is necessary to be conscious of the power of uncertainty, as uncertainty leads to discovery.

The story of James Dyson

When he started selling vacuum machines, in the late seventies, he encountered little success.

His innovation was to eliminate the paper bag, which tended to clog the engine. Then, inspiring in Mother Nature and the way the tornadoes function, the Dyson technology makes the air flow swirl inside the machine. That way, it splits between air and dust, the latter settling down in a bucket, instead of in a paper bag.

That way, the vacuum cleaner never clogs nor loses power.

Nobody showed the slightest interest in his invention.

After 15 years of relentless struggle, in 1993, he managed to produce the first machine under his own name. In a few months, he became the leader in the UK. Nowadays, one out of three British homes own a Dyson.

---

10 principles for innovation

- Ideas are fragile .
- Ideas are organic (same as the persons).
- All ideas are valuable and must be listened to.
- The creator of an idea needs help to improve it and promote it internally.
- The creator of the idea is its enforcer and should be actively involved in its further development.
- We will present our Management only the ideas that have been improved and that show potential value
- When developing an idea, we must have in mind both the technical and the marketing facets.
- The differences between people are a strength, not a weakness. We can take advantage of the possibility of interacting with people with different perspectives.
- It is sometimes wise to use the help of a go-between to facilitate the communication between people hailing from different places and cultures, or who are prone to conflict.
- The most efficient way is not always the most productive.

FLOWING

Csikszentmihalyi, a North American psychologist of Hungarian descent, has defined this condition as a particular condition of high production and enjoyment. It is about those moments where our mind flows without effort, the time when we feel concentrated on the activity just because we like it, we lose the notion of the passing of time and experience some euphoria.[8]

About those moments we can say (among other things):

- They take place when we face challenges that we can assume.
- We are absolutely concentrated on the activity.
- There are clear goals to reach.
- We forget about the risks or dangers that the activity implies.
- Lose the notion of us.
- The sense of the duration of the time is altered.
- The activity comes to constitute a purpose by itself.
- Feel certain intimate euphoria of victory.

The feelings generated under this "condition of fluency" are similar enough to what intrinsic motivation is: feeling passionately committed with the job, assuming that the job implies a positive challenge and that we can enjoy it.

Intrinsic motivation is the form of motivation that is most closely associated with creativity.

Logically, we cannot be flowing the whole day throughout, but in order to develop the creative activity it is fundamental to flow.

---

8   A few weeks ago, we read an interview to some attendees at the Olympic Mathematical Games and much to our surprise, what the math genius highlighted as the main feeling they experienced when finding the solution to a difficult problem was an exhilarating sensation, of achievement, of creativity.

And yes, maths are not something mechanical, they possess a great creativity component.

CREATE FOR THE SAKE OF CREATING

Talking about motivation, the majority of the people accept that remunerations promote a better performance.

Nevertheless, some investigations suggest that this principle is not so rigorous as is may seem. Remunerations can lower the levels of performance, especially when the performance requires creativity.

Theresa Amabile, of Brandeis's University, has realized great part of the investigation on creativity and motivation. In an experiment realized with students of basic education and of university she made two groups. To both groups she asked to realize "silly" collages. Also she asked the children to invent stories.

Those students to whom a reward had been promised brought the least creative projects, according to several of the teachers, forth. Amabile considered that the work "on order", in general, would be less creative than the work done by mere interest.

Later, Amabile asked 72 creative writers from the University of Brandeis and Boston to write some poetry. It was given to some students a list of extrinsic (external) reasons for writing poetry, like impressing the teachers, earn money and graduate in the university. It was then asked them to think about their own writings with regard to those reasons. There was given to the others a list of intrinsic reasons: the enjoyment of playing with words, satisfaction of self-expression and others. To the third group no list was given.

The results were conclusive. The students to whom the extrinsic reasons (impressing the teachers, earning money, ...) were given wrote not only in a less creative way than the others (according to the jury constituted by 12 independent poets) but the quality of their work decreased quite perceptibly.

The remunerations have, in consequence, this destructive effect especially with creative tasks, including solutions to high-level problems. I.e., the intrinsic interest in a task (something valuable of achieving for its own sake) declines when someone is rewarded for performing that task. If a remuneration (money, prizes, praises or winning a competition) happens to be seen as the reason number one "to get hooked up" by an activity, this activity will be seen as less agreeable to perform.

If we can't find our own interest in what we do, no incentive will have any effect in the outcome of our work.

In any case, incentives and perks work, but only if the person is already interested in creating or in innovating.

As a consequence, the best thing to do is creating for the sake of creating. And to enjoy it.

HAVE GOOD HUMOR

A great quantity of evidences exists on the advantages of the positive emotions, especially regarding creative tasks. All of them indicate that possessing good humor is something good if we want to be creative.

The relation between creativity and humor is very close. Both imply joining two things that do not have an obvious connection and creating a relation; escaping from a familiar scheme to adapt to another one. Sense of humor supposes creativity and ingenuity, implies a way of seeing things differently and absurdly.

The people who are in a good mood are more flexible, have a better aptitude to establish associations, to see dimensions and to detect potential relations between the stimuli than the people who are in a neutral condition.

In other words, they generate more varied ideas and combinations of those ideas, which is a crucial aspect of any creative work.

Humor, on the other hand, always implies surprise in order to be effective. It is necessary to modify the schemes and to step out of the logical and rigid structure of the vertical thinking.

Because of it, the humor is, undoubtedly, one of the characteristics of the creative people.

HUMOR AND CREATIVITY

The sense of humor is our capability to see what, despite everything, is positive in our lives and in our world.

Beyond our somber mood, we can always adopt that attitude: good humor. Humor and mood are different things altogether: it is humor that will enlighten our mood.

Good humor helps us laugh at things that otherwise would irritate us and make us aggressive or desperate; it's like an antidote that helps us be creative.

Good humor empowers some of the necessary qualities in our daily lives, such as patience and respect.

Bad humor leads us to blindness to our environment, generalizing "everything's wrong", "there is no remedy", "nothing will ever change", "I am a failure", whereas good humor helps us develop resources to face reality, analyze it and take the appropriate measures.

Physiologically, good humor accelerates our healing processes, reduces blood pressure, and increases the level of "good" hormones, activating our defense mechanisms against anxiety and anguish.

People with good humor enjoy an immunological system healthier and stronger against aggressions, whatever the kind of aggression. Laughing out loud is one of our best defenses.

Good humor also increases our self-confidence and our capacity for using our intelligence (both abstract and emotional) in the best possible way.

Enjoy

As we can see, creativity arises from curiosity and emotion and is nurtured with passion. Creativity is therefore an emotional and corporal act.[9]

It is impossible to create without a corporal suitable position (for example, can you imagine someone creating with his body standing to attention?).

Hence many of the resources and techniques that are used for promoting creativity are related to generating an emotional response: music, humor, …

Creating is enjoying.

Practice boredom

When Newton saw that apple falling to the ground, he was in an idle moment. When Archimedes discovered its famous principle, it seems that he enjoying a hot bath. When Fleming discovered penicillin, it was by mere chance (well he actually had to delve further into it a little bit more than that).

The problem is that, nowadays, "losing time", or practicing boredom, is socially poorly perceived.

Boredom is also necessary to develop the imagination, to think, to succeed and to be wrong... and without the pretension of always seeking for a "profitable" time. In the end, boredom does not guarantee the apple will fall.

---

9   **Passion**

The capacity for emotion, for enthusiasm.

When we are passionate about something, we focus exclusively on it, forgetting about anything else.

To know if we are genuinely passionate is quite easy: ¿What do you do at work, and what do you do when on holiday?

Without passion, there can be no creativity.

MEDITATION

When meditating, we sit down and focus on breathing. As the air enters and goes out of our nostrils, we focus on the sensation. When unexpected ideas come to the mind, leave them escape.[10]

American scientists have discovered that a training in this type of meditation produces a deep change in the way the brain focus its attention.

The aptitude to liberate the thoughts that arise unexpectedly in our minds allows our brain pay attention to the changes in the exterior world.

CULTIVATE HOBBIES

As we have seen, when we immerge ourselves into an exciting activity, the sensation of the passing of time gets lost and we enter a state of fluency. In that above-mentioned condition, the mind is reloaded and energized.

When we are deeply involved in an activity, we discover that we are fully focused.

Because of that, undoubtedly, it is very advisable to devote some time to our favorite hobbies. They stimulate those parts of the brain associated with the creative and positive thinking. In parallel, our self-esteem increases as well as our self-confidence.

---

10   **Pressure and deadlines**

It seems that many people feel a surge in their creativity when under a deadline pressure; that's why they procrastinate until the last moment. However, most surveys demonstrate how erroneous this is.

People are much less creative when against the clock. The pressure deriving from the oncoming of the deadline represses creativity, as we cannot immerse ourselves into the problem. We, human beings, need time to "sink" into a problem and let the ideas flow.

Whenever we give ourselves a respite in the routine, we develop new manners of thinking. Our hobbies improve creativity, help us think with more clarity and sharpen our concentration.

BE PREPARED FOR FAILURE

Undoubtedly, being creative takes its toll, and it is necessary to be prepared for it.

Opening the door to creativity means to assume that we can be wrong. And to learn also that in making mistakes we can find something valuable.

Undoubtedly, it is necessary to train if we want to extract some value from our frustrations and to experience what they generate.

QUESTION THINGS

All of us are creative. Nevertheless, in the great majority of cases this aptitude to imagine things or situations is quite linked to our life experiences, experiences that with the passing of time have been stored in our unconscious brain.

Oppugn the obvious

During the Battle of the Pacific, a Navy engineer observed the planes returning to base. The mission was very complicated. Several pilots had been shot down, and Japanese shrapnel and shots damaged the planes that made it back to base.

A bunch of mechanists was pondering the situation, aware of the fragility of the planes' hulls, suggesting to strengthen them in the places where they saw the largest holes.

The engineer, hearing those comments, addressed the mechanics and ordered them to reinforce the hulls in the areas where there were NO holes.

What was his rationale? All of the shot planes made it back to base, what demonstrated that the damages were not serious enough to prevent them from flying. Thus, strengthening the hulls in the places hit by the Japanese was not vital. What was important was to reinforce them in all the intact places.

All in all, that was the reason why the other planes didn't make it back home.

In creativity, we must see reality with new eyes, to see beyond the obvious.

Our creations are based on what already exists or has existed and they don't contribute with anything new or different. In order to contribute with innovative ideas we have to work hard in order to promote "the associated muscle".[11]

One of the first things to realize is to question the received sociocultural conditioning, in order that, little by little, we can free ourselves from the preconceived ideas about what we think to be and to know.

After going beyond the mental barriers that limit us, we will start to see things from a new perspective, much clearer and more objective. Come to this point, we are in the proper conditions to learn a series of generation of ideas techniques.

---

11   **And if...?**

Trying to imagine the practical consequences of apparently absurd statements with the question "And if ...?" will help us consider things from a new perspective, hence training our imagination.

On the other hand, this approach will help us generate new ideas upon which we can construct.

Define the problem adequately

Creativity does not blossom in wastelands. The first thing is to define the problem or difficulty that we want to analyze and solve. When choosing the problem we must have in mind a series of election criteria (implication of the people affected by the problem, benefits derived from solving that situation, simplicity of the latter, etc.).

One of the keys of creativity (and, therefore, of innovation) consists of formulating the problem adequately. The way of doing it is formulating the problem as a question. Nevertheless, this, which seems so simple, involves some complexities.

Defining the problem as specifically as possible is one of the fundamental points. It will allow us identify the important part or parts of the problem and its limits. Actually many people think that a well-enunciated problem is a solved problem.

How to formulate a problem

Once the problem chosen we must enunciate it correctly in the following form:

1. Describe the current situation and its disadvantages.
2. Identify the differences (describe the wished situation) and its advantages.
3. Make an inventory of the principal difficulties.
4. Make an inventory of the available means.

5. Formulate the objective in a sentence of maximum 20 words.
6. Challenge all of the words to see if the formulation is valid

When we have finished this process exhaustively and carefully, we will have our problem perfectly framed and defined. Then we can start acting.

Let's put a concrete example:

1. Describe the current situation and its disadvantages:
The surroundings of the housings in a residential area are degraded by the presence of rubble and garbage; and the fence is damaged. This upsets both residents and passerbies. The standing of the estate appears as poor and it proves difficult to put the apartments on sale.

2. Describe the wished situation and its advantages:
The surroundings are clean and the environment turns out to be cozy, green and lush, hence increasing the level of comfort of the inhabitants and attracting possible potential buyers.

3. Make an inventory of the principal hurdles:
- Obtain the unanimous agreement of the landlords.
- Estimate the unavoidable expenses

4. Make an inventory of all the available means:
- The motivation of half of the landlords.
- The support of the town hall.
- The level of income of the landlords allows them to cope, in principle, with some expenses.

5. Formulate the target:
To improve the standing of the housings.

6. Validate each word of the statement to make the formulation valid:

Increase the category of the housing.

THINK POSITIVELY

Actually, presenting the problems from a positive angle facilitates things very much. Let's imagine, for example, that we are looking for solutions to the traffic problem. It is much better to formulate the aim as "how can we improve the traffic" instead of "how can we avoid traffic jams".

Though in appearance the approach is similar, these are two totally differentiated forms of canalizing our creative thinking. Thinking of improving something is already a step towards improvement, it is a good mental predisposition towards the possible solutions.

Why do we imitate?

Probably our mimicking instinct is the result of millions of year of evolution, as Mother Nature is a master in imitating. There are four main reasons that trigger that instinct (all of them find their roots in evolutive psychology).

Safety: following an already existing path doesn't makes a pioneer of us, but at least we won't be devoured par wild beasts

Conformity: safety is important, but social acceptance is also important. Best example found in trends and fashion.

Conviction that the others know more than us. We focus on successful people and tend to give them more credit than they deserve.

Greed. We imitate because we desire what the other owns. It is about the fear of losing something.

RAISE THE QUESTION DIFFERENTLY

Here are the results of an investigation. When trying to eliminate a tumor in the stomach, by means of rays, without destroying the healthy tissues that surrounds the tumor, a question is asked to two different groups of people who have been assembled to generate a solution to the problem.

To the first group we tell this: " The rays can destroy the healthy tissues, how can we avoid this risk? ".

To the second group we tell this: " The healthy tissue face the risk of being destroyed; how can we protect them? ".

In the first group, 43 % of the members focused their solution on the intensity of the beams, whereas in the second one, only 14 % of people went that way.

It is evident that, as it happens in the creative processes, in the commented case the same thing happens: the way of raising the question influences the search of the solution.

So, especially when we do not see the solution to a problem, ask yourself: did I raise the question properly?

The Biro pen

As it often happens, the Biro pen was born as a solution to a problem.

In 1938, the Hungarian Laszlo Biro invented a pen that became a massive success. He got the idea during his tenure as a journalist. As he didn't write all day long, the ink tended to dry, and when having to perform an interview he had to borrow a pen because his didn't work.

When visiting a printing shop, he realized that they were capable of printing thousands of papers without staining the paper. He asked whether that huge machinery could be simplified and reduced, so we could use it in pens. The final result was the Biro, a cylinder filled with ink, with a small rotating metallic ball on the tip. With the help of gravity, the ink flew down the tube, impregnated the rotating tip, and finally the ball deposited the ink on the paper, instantly drying.

Later on, he sold his patent to Marcel Bich, a visionary entrepreneur, who made his design popular throughout the world, selling a low cost pen. In 1953, the first BIC pen was churned out from the factory.

The most relevant feature of his design, with a tungsten tip and hexagonal tube, was that it was expendable, and consequently, cheaper. Very quickly, he conquered 70% of the European market. Nowadays, every day, 15 millions of Biros are sold throughout the world.

By the way, a few years later, Bich had two other extraordinary ideas, the disposable lighters and the disposable razors. His only failure was with the disposable perfume sprays, but that's a different story altogether.

Inspired by Mother Nature

This is what the biomimetics does, it's a discipline that takes advantage of the designs created by Nature and transforms them into a source of inspiration for engineering and other sciences. It is a matter of picking those parts that can perform a concrete function.[12]

There we have the example of the planes and their model: the birds. Nowadays, planes' designing is turning its attention towards insects (the first animals that really flew). Dragon-flies, for example, fascinate scientists for their aptitude to be deceptive to their preys making them believe that they are immobile in the air (the investigators think to apply it to cam-ouflaged planes and to unmanned aircrafts); beetles, on the other hand, for their individual defensive tactic, etc.

The important thing here is to remember that the Nature always offers a good model to think about.

Velcro

One of the most famous examples of biomimetics is Velcro. This was an invention by the Swiss engineer George de Mestral when he observed that the thistle seeds clung to his dog's coat.

EXTRAPOLATE TO OTHER FIELDS

Although some previous models did exist (the first refer-ence to a corkscrew comes from England and is cited in the Agreement of the Cider, written by James Worligge in 1676), the widespread of the corkscrew takes places in the XVIIIth century, coinciding with the diffusion of the bottles made of blown glass and of the cork as the element destined to seal the bottle up to the moment of the consumption.

---

12   In the recent years, scientists have turned their attention to the capacity some lizards (the geckos) have of clinging to any kind of surface.

They are currently working on developing surgery patches that can withstand the humidity of human tissues especially around the heart or the intestines, and nevertheless retain their suturing capability.

This is a good example of biomimetics.

With the imposition of the metallic spiral as a basic element for the extraction of corks, the evolution of the corkscrew centered on the development of the most comfortable method to realize the operation, i.e., in the development of the handle and the mechanical system.

Corkscrew with a T frame with a spiral, leverage corkscrew, etc. They are some of the uncountable models designed in different epochs.

Nevertheless, the most renowned is a version of the lever corkscrew that developed Herber Allen, an American oil tycoon, fond of inventions. This man, in 1979, invented the corkscrew Screwpull.

The invention had its foundation in applying the system of perforation in oilrigs to the extraction of corks in a bottle of wine.

The Screwpull corkscrew is already a classic amongst connoisseurs.

Challenging questions

Why do we assume that clocks and watches are to be sold in a jewelry store? This was the challenging question a clock company faced when they decided to enter the Indian market, back in the eighties. They wondered how they could enter the market when they realized that a competitor already monopolized the usual channels.

When trying to give an answer to that question, they detected that their target customers were also customers of appliance or department stores.

That company decided to install independent booths in department stores o retailers.

Today, they are leaders in the Indian market.

Linking different knowledge

This one is a technique very important in creativity, and also very useful.

A while ago, we read an article about the increasing links between mathematics and ... biology!

In effect, lately, with the so known as system biology, we have to handle an enormous quantity of information that the biologist cannot control. Hence he is in need of mathematical models pointing him towards which are the fundamental parameters in the internal machinery of the living cell, because they might point at a certain gene as a more probable candidate for producing a certain effect.

Challenges

One of the most powerful triggering mechanisms for creativity is identifying a challenge.

Some decades ago, during an informal conversation, when observing a kneeling maid cleaning the floor, somebody quipped to his interlocutor, a military engineer "Why don't you invent something useful for the people, instead of that nasty stuff for military airplanes?".

Manuel Jalón, that was his name, took the gauntlet. The way he recounts it, during his numerous trips to the USA, he had noticed some large containers used for washing up the warehouses. Then in 1956, he had the idea of taking a broomstick, attaching some spongeous stripes to it, and then using a bucket with some drying rolls on top of it. That artifact allowed people washing floor while standing.

Later he got it patented under the name "fregona", and with few changes, it remained that way until nowadays.

Once again, despite that we are talking of a revolutionary invention, and a boon to mankind, the beginnings were dire, as people deemed it as useless. Fortunately, the tourists that visited Spain at that time, found it most practical and bought them with enthusiasm, hence eventually helping in its wide spreading.

New approaches, different approximations from very different fields. Swapping points of view so we can see different things.

To know our Personal style (and others')

In spite of all of the above, there are several authors who underline the particular way of facing creativity depending on the people. They talk about "creative styles". Actually no style is better than another, simply each one has its particularities.

When working with other people and thinking about creativity it is important to have these styles in account. Knowing in depth the peculiarities of every style allows us estimate the contributions that each of the styles can put forward.

Visionary style

They feel comfortable focusing on the final result, on a vision of what we aim to create, they imagine an ideal outcome and then allows these goals guide us for moving on. Using this style can provide direction and impetus to a team.

The people with this style look first for ideas and intuitions that lead them to decisions on the long-term objectives, they use the creative process to find innovations that reach those aims. This style can be defined as idealistic.

Modificator style

The people who prefer this style feel comfortable modifying and building onto what's already known, onto real and proven things. They like to move forward step by step. They provide the team with the necessary stability and the meticulousness to do a quality work.

They are people who also look, first, for facts. They use the creative process to find innovations they can construct upon and improve in an active form what has already been done in the past. A word to describe the modifying style is constructor.

Experimenter style

They like to experiment with a trustworthy process to evaluate combinations of different and new ideas. They contribute to a team by combining the information of the whole group to ensure a solution of consensus and feasibility.

Those people look first for facts and pay special attention to the information that needs yet to be gathered. They use the creative process to find solutions that can be verified and that we can learn from, with information from many sources. As a synonymous to this style we can use the word combiner.

Exploratory style

They like to explore, to work in the unknown and the unpredictable. This style enjoys using symbols and metaphors to come to new ideas. They contribute to the team by questioning the assumptions and the basic "paradigms".

Those people look first for ideas that defy the conventional assumptions. They use the creative process to find innovations that are based on new assumptions and perceptions. They like to discover.[13]

---

13 **The clumsy balance between risk and boldness**

Quite often, the so-called celebrities are so focused on being original that they don't have time enough for being creative.

The unavoidable quality for being creative is boldness, fleeing from common sense; having the intellectual courage to take decisions, making yourself strong to face a social pressure always too conservative.

And all of that without exaggerating, and finding the right balance between risk and boldness; the same as the Japanese fish "fugu" gourmets.

In Japan, you can eat "fugu" meat, which is extremely venomous unless if carefully dished. The most refined chefs leave the faintest quantity of poison in the fish that blemishes the lips, to remind the customers how close to death hey have traveled.

Well, even that way, every year, there are still a few customers who travel too far and end up dead before the end of the dinner.

2

CREATIVITY TECHNIQUES

The creativity techniques are methods that support the creative training. All of them imply certain actions that, in general, are more important than the technique itself and that act as a stimulus.

A creative technique is something that should ensure some kind of "creative", original and different results. The usefulness of any creative technique dwells in that it allows us focus the brain towards thinking in concrete steps or procedures.

The principal mission of the techniques that foment creativity is to help us break our mental wiring and to discover new paths leading to the solution of problems.

Actually, the idea of using a creativity technique is to rescue people from the "old habits" and give them a different point of view, to force them do something that they would normally not do. This explains why something at first glance somewhat irrelevant as a technique can yield good results. The creativity techniques are not creative by themselves; it is the people, as they incorporate them, creating new associations, with a new vision, that obtain a creative outcome.

The utilization of techniques is not always successful, but they help us reach some objectives that are supposed close to creativity. Actually, as we have mentioned, they allow our brain work in concrete stages or procedures. I.e., on one hand, they allow us follow an established order to achieve a wished aim and, on the other one, help us dismantle the structure of the usual vertical thinking.

When we pick a creative method or technique, we accept the fulfillment of certain steps. These are actually the steps that organize the disorganization where we enter when thinking "creatively".

Without any doubt these techniques must be put into practice, but, due to the immense quantity and variety of existing creative methods, it is important to have a very clear idea about which is the most convenient technique for us according to the situation that we face.

The explanation that, later, we give for every technique contributes to define perfectly which is its aim and for what purpose it is possible to concretely use that technique. I.e., let's first think about where we want to travel.

Before entering some classification model, we consider pertinent to explain the basic characteristics of the most used techniques, establishing the principal aspects taken in account to establish our classification.

The creative techniques belong to two main areas:[14]

- Techniques based on the process: Its principal aim is to achieve that the thinking process, whether in-group or individual, work in a way different from the traditional one. They are characterized by being orientated to the people more than to the objects (or products) to create.
- Techniques centered on the product: the establishment of a heuristic methodology, which implies applying a

---

14   Despite the virtually limitless quantity of suitable techniques (creativity, by essence has no boundaries), in many organizations, although they are keen to accept "new ways of thinking", people tend to stick to a couple of techniques. The reason is because of the past experiences with the aforementioned techniques. Anybody fixing a situation with the help of a certain technique will tend to include it in his natural way of tackling problems.

system of analysis to a universe of objects or concepts that leads to enunciate all the possible organizations of the above-mentioned universe characterizes them.

Another taxonomy or classification, very commonly seen in the different manuals on creativity, organizes the creative techniques using analogical methods (those that use the evocative and creative power of the metaphor); in random or serendipitous methods (those that foment an attitude of provocation of interpretable relations in terms of new suggestions, such as "lateral thinking" from Edward De Bono's, and that support a vision reconciled with failures as a source of inspiration), and in antithetic methods (methods where we force the contrast of the elements into their more contradictory aspects in order to break the conventions on their perception).[15]

In any case, a classification is just a way of organizing things. Actually, talking about creativity seems antithetic. Because of what we were saying a few paragraphs above is that the creativity techniques are as numerous as our imagination wishes to be.

15   We personally think that creativity and inspiration are always about group work. An idea that is not shared simply doesn't exist. Ideas exist when they are shared and explained. The myth of the lonesome genius is basically that, a myth. Just try to conduct a brainstorming on your own …

Six hats for one single head

This method relates to the way our thoughts can be redirected with the use of certain gimmicks. The most popular is called the 6 hats methods, but we can think of any other object or image in order to trigger a specific style of thinking in our brains.

This method designed by the Maltese psychologist and physiologist Edward de Bono, is a simple but effective procedure that allows us find and manage new ideas, both individually and in-group.

It is about the fact that people use different types of thinking when physically putting on a hat of a certain color. The idea of putting on a certain hat implies assuming and acting under the role established by the above-mentioned hat.

This process allows us avoid repetitive discussions and misunderstandings. Besides, it allows us take advantage of the talent of all the involved people. As well, it allows us go "beyond" the most apparent solutions and makes possible to find effective and simple answers, which are not always obvious.

The colors and associations of the hats are the following ones:

White hat:

The white hat implies neutrality and objective behavior. The thinker with a white hat on puts forward neutral terms of reference, which must not be used for supporting a specific point of view. With this hat we accept neither our own opinion, nor the forebodings, nor the judgments based on experience or on intuitions. This hat talks only about facts and there are excluded, therefore, the opinions, the feelings, the impressions, the forebodings, etc.

The energy of this hat is destined to seek and expose information. Because of it, in general, this hat is used initially in a creative session.

RED HAT:

This hat offers the opportunity to express emotions, feelings and unrational aspects (hunches, intuitions, sensations). With this hat it is not needed to explain or to justify our feelings (actually, this should not be allowed when wearing this hat).

The objective of this hat is to make the emotional background visible in order to observe its influence. The hat is always applied to a specific idea or situation.

The aim of the red hat is to express feelings as they arise, without forcing any judgment. In fact, with this technique it is not necessary to guess the feelings of the others. We have a way of directly asking for them.

Because with this background decisions are adopted and plans can unfold, occasionally it can be useful to imagine a different emotional background and see how different things could be.

BLACK HAT:

The black hat is, in the traditional thinking the most used of them all. It is the hat of precaution, of survival, of critical thinking. It includes the negative aspects, the gloom, and the pessimistic vision. It implies critical judgment, the "this will never work".

The black hat thinking is always logical. Because of that, whatever we express with this hat on has to make sense and be reasonable (otherwise that might belong, for example, to the red hat).

This hat turns out to be very useful in the valuation of an idea and in its planning.

YELLOW HAT:

The yellow hat is luminous, optimistic and involves the positive aspects of a suggestion. It centers on the tentative benefits and implies using constructive thinking.

It is probably the hat most hard to wear and to which we are less accustomed. This hat forces us look for the value of an idea, and generate alternative approaches to a problem. In other words, this hat implies triggering an attitude that makes us being hopefully positive in relation to a situation. It is a hat of opportunities.

When someone uses this hat, the judgments have to be logical and rational, because otherwise they would be occurring in the area of the red hat.

GREEN HAT:

The green hat is the hat of energy. Putting it on implies creativity and new ideas. This hat therefore looks for alternatives, raises possibilities. It goes beyond the already known, the obvious and the satisfactory. It generates provocation in order to step out of our habitual guidelines of thinking.

The green hat has to deal with new ideas and new manners of looking at things. Putting it on implies reserving a time for the deliberate creative thinking.

Therefore, this hat demands new ideas, new approaches and more alternatives. Obviously, with this hat judgments are not allowed.

The underlying idea of this hat is the belief that there is always more than one way of doing things, as always more than one response exists. Therefore, to a certain extent, the green hat seeks constant improvement.

BLUE HAT:

This hat is like a conductor. It relates to the control and organization of the thinking process. It rules over other hats as it exercises the control (metathinking). It focuses the thinking.

The blue hat gives us a global vision. It indicates us when to swap hats. If we are developing a formal process, this hat controls the protocol. Besides organizing the other hats, this hat organizes other aspects of the thinking: the evaluation of priorities or the enumeration of restrictions. In sum, the blue hat impersonates the coordinator of the meeting. The best expert in the technique is the one that should always wear this hat.

The distinctive characteristic of the six hats technique is to simplify the thinking process, i.e., to differentiate between the emotional, optimistic, logical, pessimistic aspects, etc., hereby modifying the traditional style of thinking that uses to approach situations without differentiating the points of view. With this technique, on the other hand, we look at the different points of view one by one.

On the other hand, the six hats technique allows us decode situations, as the ideas are analyzed from different points of view, from different types of thinking and putting into play several different roles.

It allows us study an idea and analyzes it thoroughly, which implies identify its strong and weak points and their degree of viability.

On the other hand, with this technique (as with so many others that are approached in this book) thinking becomes a game instead of being a situation of pressure and conditioning.

BRAINSTORMING

It is the best-known creative method. But it is as famous as erroneously used. This method is also known by the name of rain of ideas, whirlwind of ideas, storm of ideas, triggering of ideas, verbal mobilization, ideas bombing, jolt of brains, promotion of ideas, cerebral storm, triggering of ideas, avalanche of ideas, tempest in the brain and tempest of ideas.

The method developed by Alex Osborn (specialist in creativity and advertising) in the 30s, began in the area of the companies, being applied to topics as productivity, with the need to find new ideas and solutions for the products in the market, to find new methods that develop creative thinking... at all levels.

It is a method for generating ideas in-group. It is a way of achieving that a group generates a great number of ideas in not too much time.[16]

---

16   **The pearl diver**
Imagine a pearl diver in the Andaman Islands. He gets on board of his pirogue and starts rowing across the lagoon. When he decides of a good spot, he dives headfirst, collects an oyster from the seabed, emerges for fresh air, climbs onto the pirogue, rows back ashore and opens the oyster.
As he doesn't find any pearl, he steps back into the pirogue and there he goes again rowing back across the lagoon.
What a waste of time! What's reasonable is to not come back ashore until the pirogue is full of oysters, and only then row back ashore.
Pearls are very scarce and a diver has to open a large amount of them before finding a single pearl.

The phases that a "brainstorming" must have (ideally) are the following ones:

Warming-up phase: In this phase the group practices to reach a better collective functioning and to activate the neuronal interconnections of the creative process. As an example for warming up, for example, we could name all the things that can be used as a hat.

Phase of ideas generation: Before formally initiating this phase we must find, first, a minimal number of ideas we want to find (for example 150) and we decide the time we are going to work (for example, 10 minutes).

During this phase four fundamental rules exist:

Any critique is forbidden (including self-criticism), whatever negative or positive. There is a time to generate ideas and another time to value them and to evaluate them.

Any idea is welcome. Any occurrence, image or recollection must be expressed without deeming it: obvious, insignificant, immoral or ridiculous. Any idea has to be written or drawn without self-censoring. Free imagination is promoted. The ideas do not have to be necessarily realistic.

Generate the largest quantity of possible ideas without analyzing their quality. The quantity of ideas is very important due to the fact that in advance it is not possible to know which one of the ideas can be selected, in order to later, solve a problem or find a new solution.

That's the same situation when talking about ideas production. Many a time we produce one or two ideas and gleefully assume that they are the answer we were expecting. But creative ideas are like pearls, they are rare.

So, what's wise is to produce as many ideas as we can before deciding about which ones are the good ones.

The development and association of ideas is desirable. It allows us develop, transform or modify the ideas of the others. This effect is technically named as "selective resonance".

Generally, we tend to record our ideas in writing and, actually, we annotate them in a strict chronological order as soon as they pop up. In this stage it is indispensable not to identify the person who has formulated a specific idea. The ideas, once emitted, do not have any owner. [17]

When the group reaches the number of ideas that has been fixed as the target or has consumed the scheduled time, the ideas are numbered and qualified before entering the evaluation stage.

After the stage of generation of ideas, the group establishes the criteria to evaluate them. For example: economic profitability, degree of feasibility, and possible extension of the idea…

A possibility for evaluating the ideas might be to consider them (by means of a punctuation) according to a series of conditions or previously established requirements, which they must satisfy.

In any case, about the moment of the evaluation we agree:

- To analyze the strong points of the idea and then pay attention to the weak points.
- To be attentive to the novel aspects of the options.
- Don't lose of sight the initial target (the problem or creative challenge to solve).

---

17 **Creativity and colors**

A recent survey published in Science gives us some hints about how color does affect our performance. For a productive brainstorming, blue seems to be the winning color. This is because for most of the surveyed people, blue relates to peace and openness; two vital conditions for triggering creativity.

Rules for a good "brainstorming"

- Say everything that comes across your mind (whatever it is relevant or irrelevant)
- Include even obvious things (it is possible that they are obvious only to you)
- Don't interrupt the flow of ideas
- Don't be bothered by repetitions
- Do not explain or justify yourself
- Avoid judgments of value
- Does not matter to add an idea that another people should have suggested
- Accept and enjoy the moments of silence - they allow more ideas to be generated
- Be irrational
- Risk: toss ideas without second thoughts!

... READY, STEADY, GO!

ANALOGIES

It is about linking, about connecting or creating bridges between different worlds. For this, it is possible to go from the concrete to the abstract or from the abstract to the concrete. It is applied to the object which logic we want to modify (the rules or characteristics), of to a different object. What we want to modify, the experts call it "metaphoricaled object" or "analogicaled object", whereas the object we use as a source for ideas for the modification they name it "metaphoricalling object".

There are diverse techniques that use analogies, which is a process of applying to an object, concept or situation that we want to modify, the logic or characteristics of a different object (concept or situation).

A very common technique is Sinectics (W. Gordon) that uses analogies and metaphors as a systematical way to change the frame of reference when seeking the solution of a problem.

The Sinectics process includes two basic aspects: relative to transforming what's strange into something familiar, and also transforming what's familiar into something strange.

- Turning what's strange into something familiar. It consists of distorting, or inverting the usual ways of seeing what makes our world a safe and familiar place. It is a deliberate attempt to achieve a new vision of the world, of the people, of the ideas, of the feelings and of the things that we know. In order to turn what's known into something strange we can use diverse mechanisms of metaphorical character. [18]

- Turning what's familiar into something strange. In any situation where a problem appears and a solution is tried, the responsibility of the involved people is to understand the problem. This is an analytical phase where must be explored all the ramifications and foundations of the problem

All this is achieved, essentially, through four analogical mechanisms, which are described below.

1. Direct Analogies: two facts, products or situations are compared. (What exists in the nature that looks like this problem? For example, compare shampoo with instantaneous coffee).

2. Personal Analogies: it consists of identifying ourselves with the parts of the problem ("how would the problem feel if it was human?"). Personal analogy requires empathy, in order to reach the level where we lose ourselves and acquire the maximum possible things of the other part. We emphasize the importance of the distance (the more the better) to the object. Gordon, one of its creators, distinguishes four levels. Let's imagine that someone wants to achieve empathy with a plane:

   A. Description of known facts: the subject states he has wings.

   B. Identification of common emotions: the subject feels untouchable as nobody can reach it.

   C. Empathic identification with something alive: in our example the object is inanimate.

---

18   For instance, in the world of finance, there are many hydraulic analogies (no clue why): flood the market, liquidity, liquid assets, refloat a business, cash flow, underwater economy, etc.

D. Empathic identification with something inanimate: the subject expresses his impotence for being deprived of freedom.

3. Symbolic Analogies: we try to describe the problem with a global image that shows it from another point of view ("If our problem was a book, what title would it have?"). Another example: if we propose to improve the flow of information from the top of the organization downwards throughout all the levels, we might compare it with the leaves of a tree that in autumn, fall down from the branches down to the ground.

4. Fantastic Analogies: here the problem moves to an ideal world, where restrictive conditions do not exist, to return later to the concrete world with new ideas. ("How would we wish that this was working?"). Another concrete example: we can ask us what would happen if the information flow in our organization were telepathic.

The distinctive aspect of this creative technique is that it links the totally different logics of two objects, concepts or situations.

The technique is very useful for meetings and discussions about problems solving, for improving the quality of the processes inside the company, for adapting the distinctive characteristics of a market or organization to others aspects, that, at least seemingly, do not have an actual relation. All this allows us understand something that we do not know using something we know better.

Example: "What would happen if a dishwasher looked like an oven microwave?; what would happen if watching television was like reading a magazine?", etc. The disciplined use of analogy often helps us focus on problems long last forgotten, and shows us a path towards innovative solutions.

GUIDELINES FOR PRACTICING SYMBOLIC ANALOGIES

Process
- Define what we want to achieve.
- Select a symbol.
- Name and to describe the characteristics of the symbol.
- Generate specific ideas on how to solve a problem realizing associations between the characteristics of the selected symbol and the problem.
- Share the best ideas with the rest of the group.

GUIDELINES FOR PRACTICING SYMBOLIC ANALOGIES

Completed example

A - Brief description of what we want to achieve
i.e. "Improve the communication policy at the office"

B - Symbol (here a pencil) selected to illustrate the description

Characteristics of the symbol (3)
- Different components
- Eraser attached
- The components fit together well
- It writes in all the positions
- It writes the messages with care

Specific ideas across associations (4)

- Include all the departments in the creation of the policy
- Give everybody the permission to commit mistakes
- Express yourself with politeness
- The communication systems have to work in different directions

METAPHORS

The metaphor is, probably, the dynamical nucleus of the creative thinking and one of the basic functioning principles of our brain. When we meet something unknown, our first reflex is to try to connect it with something already known.

If we stop to ponder, we define the reality metaphorically in all the aspects of our life and, later, we act according to metaphors.

A metaphor is a thinking technique that connects two universes different in their meanings. The most common metaphors use images. No metaphor is enough to embrace reality or a concept. It just emphasizes some aspects and conceals some others.

The way in which we describe something can affect the way we perceive it and, in turn, the way we use it.

The metaphor is based on a relation by analogy, which goes from the abstract to the concrete. It shares with the analogy the mental operation of similarity between two elements. It differs from symbolism, where we go from the concrete, the represented, to the abstract; whereas the metaphor, as we have already said, travels from abstract to concrete.

For example: the food chain, the flow of time, etc.

The key to metaphorical thinking is similarity. The mind tends to look for similarities.

A roadmap, for example, is a model or a metaphor of reality and it is tremendously useful for us.

The interest of the metaphor is enormous: it forces us look for analogies; i.e. it connects objects or situations that at first glance are different or distant.

The metaphor, in consequence, supposes stepping out of the established frame. Because of it is so useful as a creative method.

Before any challenge, looking for metaphors possibly constitutes an exercise that crushes the mind and discovers unexpected resources.

List of ideas for metaphors

Here comes a list of ideas. Select one or more ideas from the list and compare them with your problem. Produce all the similarities and connections you can make between each comparison. For example, what has to do "cutting this year budget" with "swimming underwater" or with "central heating".

To climb a mountain	To conduct an orchestra
To prepare a cocktail	To drive a car
To take a bath	To paint the house
To mount in bicycle	To sell encyclopedias
To bungee jump	To sail
To swim underwater	To write a mail
To play an instrument To sunbath	
To win a competition	To assemble a tent
To iron	To walk the dog
To marry	To see a movie
To plan a dinner	To break glasses
To write a book	To wash dishes
To read a novel	To garden
To cook	To go fishing
To play tennis	To change the diapers

Mental maps

"Mind mapping" is a tool developed by the British psychologist Tony Buzan at the beginning of the 70s. The importance of the mental maps takes its root in that they constitute an expression of a form of thinking: the radiating thinking. The mental map is a graphical technique that gives us access to the potential of the brain in a most creative way.

Its effect is immediate: it helps organize projects in a few minutes, stimulates creativity, overcomes the obstacles inherent to the written medium and offers an effective method for the production and exchange of ideas.

The mental map bears in mind the way the brain gathers, processes and stores information. Its structure registers a visual image that facilitates us extract information, annotate and memorize it with facility.

We might summarize the definition of mental maps with these words:

A graphical representation of an integral process that facilitates the capture of notes and effective revisions. It allows us unify, separate and integrate concepts in order to analyze and to synthesize them, sequentially; in a structure increasingly organized, consisted of a set of images, colors and words, which mimics the processes of linear and spatial thinking.

To elaborate a mental map we start with a word or a main idea; then we associate – 5 to 10 main ideas related to it. Then we take again each of those words and to each of them we associate 5 to 10 main words related to each of those terms. And so on and so on.

- Creative, central and unforgettable idea.
- Secondary ideas written in thinner branches.
- A color for each different informative block.
- The map is read clockwise.
- We use key words (adjectives, nouns, verbs).
- A word per line written in upper case. The word is annotated on the line.
- A symbol per idea.
- Uses colors and images with creativity.
- Different Letters (form and size).
- Symbols, Codes, Arrows.

Although the technique has multiple uses, its principal application in the creative process is the exploration of the problem (to have different perspectives of it) and also in the generation of ideas.

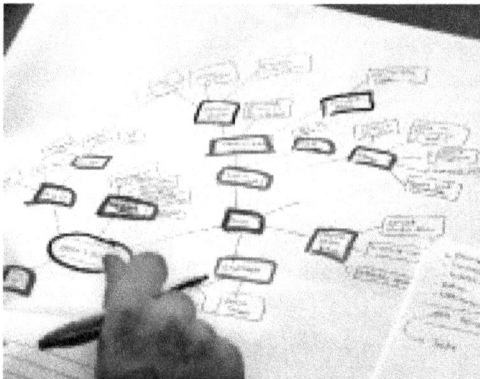

COMBINATORIAL TABLES

This technique tries to find previously unseen relations and elaborate new ones.

Despite the fact that, in some way, it looks like the previous technique, here elements are not used as a stimulus, but are specifically related to the characteristics of our problem.

In this case we construct a table which columns will be constituted by material components or elements that form our problem or product.

The rows of the table will enumerate the different characteristics or ways of realizing the components previously identified.

Finally, we will analyze every intersection between columns and rows to detect new ideas.

Continuing with the example of the shampoo previously used:

	Flask	Perfume	Color	Labels
Transparent				
Fruity				
Floral				

The combination flask - fruit tree might generate the idea of a flask with the form of a fruit. The combination labels -transparent suggests us the idea of engraving the name of the shampoo on the flask.

As the table is being completed and we establish the relations, new ideas appear, which, beyond their applicability, lead to a reflection on perspectives that otherwise may have been overlooked.

This technique is useful:

- To find aspects of the problem not previously taken in account
- The creation of new products or services.
- The creation of new lines of an existing product.
- To promote aspects of the product or service that were not born in mind initially.

Classifying ideas

A major cement company, during a session of creative thinking about prepared concrete, generated 250 ideas, which they classified into four main (and quite surprising) categories:

* Stars: great and clearly valuable ideas that can be put into practice immediately.

* Balls: valuable ideas that we have to ponder about during some time in order to see if they are practical.

* Apples: good ideas for progressive improvements, and that we can put into practice quickly.

* Bones: Ideas that may look interesting, but that after closer scrutiny, have little meat on the bone.

From the 250 presented ideas, emerged 10 stars amongst which was a new way of elaborating prefabricated elements. That solution allowed the contractors double the performance they obtained from their investments in moulds for those prefab elements.

Asking questions

There are many authors who underline that questioning is the most creative of the human behaviors. Developing a series of questions can be very useful in the exploration of a problem.

This list of questions is used for formulating all the possible approaches, and hereby, for opening the perspective that we have of the problem. They are also useful for the perception of new uses, applications or possibilities of a product or a service.[19]

List of questions
When? What class of? With what?
Why? Which? In what?
What? For which? Does it bring over of what?
By means of what? With whom? Of what?
What class of? Wherefrom? Towards where?
Why? For what reason? In how much time?
To whom? From whom? More?
For whom? How? More often?
Who? In what measure? Less?

---

19   Rudyard Kipling used to stress the importance of questioning: "*Six honest servants told me what I know: what, how, when, where, why and who*". After asking those questions, and getting the answers, we have a clearer and wider perspective of the problem, and we can start with the following stage, the stage of ideas generation.

All? How much?
Not all? To what distance? Why?
Importantly? Where? Whence?
Again? In another place? More difficult?
How many times?

The "five whys" technique

Let's analyze the classical case of some Japanese manufacturers in the seventies.

They adopted the habit of asking "why" five times when they were discovering an important problem in production or distribution, as they believed that the actual reasons were at least four levels below the surface.

Example:

1) Why did the machine stop?
   A fuse was burned by an overload

2) Why was there an overload?
   There was no sufficient lubricant in the bearings

3) Why was there no sufficient lubricant?
   The bomb was not pumping enough

4) Why was the pump not pumping sufficient lubricant?
   The axle of the pump was vibrating as result of the attrition

5) Why was there attrition?
   There was no filter, what allowed metallic particles enter the pump

The installation of a filter solved the problem.

Ideas stimulators

Emerson has demonstrated that "the creating skill is the adapting skill". Here you can find some questions that can be used as a springboard to find other ideas. Change, adapt, add or erase what is necessary.

1. WHO

      * who can help me realize contributions?
      * to whom must I sell this idea?
      * who can help me get additional resources?
      * who will benefit of it?

2. WHAT

      * what do I need to get additional resources?
      * what techniques or methods can I use?
      * which is the best way?
      * which is the first step?
      * what will make them buy it?

3. WHERE

      * where must I begin?
      * where can we find resistances?
      * where must I plant seeds?

4. WHEN

* when must I present the plan?
* when must I implement the ideas?
* when must we check our strategy?

5. WHY

* why should they buy this idea?
* why is this the best way?
* why is resistance so strong?

6. HOW

* how can we improve this idea?
* how we can test it?
* how can I persuade the people with influence?

SCAMPER

This creative technique consists of using a list of questions that stimulate the generation of ideas. Alex Osborn, the creator of brainstorming, established the first ones. Later they were arranged for Bob Eberle into the acronym that gives its name to the technique:

S: Substitute?
C: Combine?
A: Adapt?
M: Modify?
P: Propose for other uses?
E: Eliminate or to reduce to the minimum?
R: Reorganize?/invert?

The SCAMPER technique is based on the belief that everything new is somewhat an addition or modification of something that already exists.

Here we need to have perfectly established what is the problem. Once done this, we can use SCAMPER.

- To substitute. (To replace things, places, procedures, people, ideas...)
- To combine (to combine topics, concepts, ideas, emotions ...)
- To adapt (to adapt ideas from other contexts, times, schools, people ...)

- To modify (to add something to an idea or a product, to transform it)
- To propose for other uses (to extract the secret possibilities of things)
- To eliminate (to remove concepts, parts, elements of the problem)
- To reorder (or to invert elements, to swap places, roles...)

Later on comes the evaluation of the generated ideas. Previously, it is interesting to have agreed upon some common criteria.

Actually, this technique can be used along with other techniques in the divergent process of generation of ideas.

Steps to perform SCAMPER

- Identify the product or service to process.
- Apply each of the verbs in the checklist to suggest changes in the product or service.
- Make sure to ask each and all of the action questions
- Check the changes to determine which are the best adapted according to the initial criterion of solution.

SCAMPER

TO SUBSTITUTE?
Who can be more likely replaced?
What else can be replaced?
Can we change the rules?
Other ingredients?
Other materials?
Another process or procedure?
Another place?
A different approach?

TO COMBINE?
What ideas can be combined?
Can we combine intentions?
What about a collection?
What about a mix, an alloy, a group?
To combine units?
What other articles might we mix with this one?
How might we pack a combination?
What is it possible to combine to multiply the possible uses?
What materials might we combine?

TO ADAPT?
What else looks like this?
What another idea does it suggests you?
Does our past offer us some parallelism?
What might we copy?
What might we emulate?
What idea might we incorporate?
What another process might we adapt?
What else might we adapt?
In which different contexts can I include my concept?
What ideas from other fields, different from mine, can I incorporate?

TO PROPOSE?
What can we propose, extend, or extend?
What can we exaggerate?
What can we oversize?
What can we add?
More time? Louder?
Higher?
Longer?
With more frequency?
Additional characteristics?

What can give added value?
Can we duplicate it?

TO MODIFY?

How do we alter it to improve it?
Is it possible to modify?
There is some peculiarity?
To change the meaning, the color, the movement, the sound, the smell, the form, the size?
To change the name?
Other changes?
What changes do we do in the blueprints?
In the process?
In the marketing?
What another form might it take?
Another packaging?
Might we combine the packaging with the object?

OTHER USES FOR IT?

Other uses if we modify it?
What more things could it do?
Other extensions?
Other markets?

TO ELIMINATE OR TO MINIMIZE?

What would happen if it were smaller?
What would there be necessary to omit?
Would I have to divide it? Split it?
To split it in different parts?
To reduce? To make more efficient?
To do it in miniature?
To condense?
To compact?
To conserve?

To eliminate?
Can rules be eliminated?
What is that it is not necessary?
What would a drawing of the process reveal?

TO REORGANIZE?
What other organizations might do better?
To swap components?
A different model?
A different distribution?
Another sequence?
To change the order?
Switch cause and effect?
To change the speed? The pace?
To change the planning?

TO INVERT?
Can I swap positive and negative?
What are the opposites?
What are the negatives?
Can we spin it?
Can we flip it?
What's above instead of below?
What's below instead of above?
Consider it retrospectively?
Invert the roles?
To do what is not expected?

Revertion

Also called technique "of the opposite". The publicist Alex Osborn, inventor of the brainstorming, enunciated several principles and creativity techniques. One of them is Revertion.

Reverting is about putting the structure, the elements, the functions, the utilization or the position of an object upside-down. It is the technique of "vice versa" or of juggling with opposite elements.

This way, a very interesting exercise in creativity, consists in creating the anti-object or opposite object in its form or functions.

What would be the anti-object of an umbrella? A parasol, a funnel, a floating anchor, a colander, a shower, a bellows, a parachute, a candle...

The steps for this technique are the following ones:

1. Formulate the problem clearly
2. List the elements that constitutes the situation (what characterizes the situation and why?)
3. Pick one o more of those elements and mention its opposite.
4. Formulate the following question: "How to do...?" And then leave the ideas flow.
5. Finally, it is necessary to transform these ideas into its opposite in order to obtain solutions to the initial problem.

Example

Problem: Achieving that the members of my team express their views more freely during meetings.

1. List the elements that constitute the situation:
"What characterizes the meeting?"
Meeting: tables, chairs, agenda, light, room, entertainer.
"What's the purpose?"
To exchange ideas, to decide, to organize...

2. Election of one of the elements: to exchange ideas.

3. The opposite: not to exchange ideas.

4. What is it necessary to not exchange ideas?
- To keep silence
- To criticize the others,
- Silence, the boss speaks,
- To forget the hour of the meeting, ...

5. When the time has passed, we stop the process and we transform the obtained ideas into their opposite.
To remain silent : to talk, to dare to talk
To criticize the others: to wait until the others finish before expressing ourselves; thinking in them positive aspects, respect them
Hush, the boss's talking the chief is the facilitator of the meeting and lets everybody express. The boss does not censure "bad ideas"
To forget meeting time to respect the meeting schedule, to be punctual. To find time to be available.

In one of the Aesop's fables, a crane bird was longingly staring at a long neck flask. The bird wanted to drink from the flask, but the water level was too low for that.

The bird started thinking about how to extract the water from the jar but he could not come up with any solution.

Eventually, the bird shifted paradigms: instead of looking for means of extracting water, he thought of introducing things in the jar, so the water level would go up.

So he started dropping stones in the jar until he could reach the water with his beak.

LOOKING FOR FLAWS

Many ideas arise from mere current dissatisfactions, i.e., when a problem exists (the best and simplest definition about "problem" is a "difference between what we have and what we want to have").

They are many people who think that perfection is a blockade and that it is imperfection, the unfinished thing, the untidy thing that stimulates inventiveness and creativity.

The creative technique called "looking for flaws" is about enumerating, Actually, the flaws we find in objects, behaviors, instruments or institutions and, later, classifying them.

The following step is to split the flaws between those that can have a solution and those that cannot.

LIST OF ATTRIBUTES

This technique seeks to generate creative ideas with the aim in mind of modifying and improving any product, service or process.

We identify the attributes of a product, service or process, with the purpose of considering them to be a source of modification and development.

We can make lists of physical characteristics, of uses, of synonymous, of antonyms, of parts, of connotations, etc.

The attributes can be so numerous that their treatment becomes difficult, which forces us to reduce their number. For this, the method distinguishes the essential attributes from the trivial ones, to stick only to the former.

The procedure for this technique consists of picking - first - the product, service or process to improve or the problem to resolve.

Once done this, it is a matter of identifying its physical components, of describing the functions of every element in terms of attributes, of realizing an analysis of the attributes, with the purpose of deciding which ones are essential and which ones are trivial. Sometimes, we may consider them as definitively good, whereas others may be clearly improvable. The attention, logically, focus on the latter.

Later on, we take every attribute and we think about the way of changing or improving it. For each attribute, we might actually make a SCAMPER. We must make a systematical analysis of all the opportunities of improvement for every attribute, trying all the ideas that seem suitable, until no further possibility remains. This is the eminently creative phase, where it is necessary to use our imagination thoroughly.

The efficiency of this technique becomes clearer in those problems where we can split their elements into concrete and definite attributes. If we talk about a canned product, we might consider the attributes: form, color, sealing system, materials, illustration, text, etc.

On the other hand, when it is a matter of improving processes, it turns out to be more difficult to identify the attributes, though the method remains applicable.

The List of Attributes is a good starting point for the analytical - combinatorial methods [20]

LIST OF ATTRIBUTES N º 1
Height
Width
Color
Components
Date
Distance
Duration
Structure
State
Status
Fact of
Reliability
Flexibility
Depth
Form

---

20   Of course, there are pre-existing lists. Attached are a couple of examples. However it is always better to create our own list, although we can get some inspiration from an already existing one.

Strength
Frequency
Identifying
Importance
Place
Measurement
Origin
Weight
Position
Owner
Quantity
Quantity
Alike
Time
Texture
Type
Speed
Volume

LIST OF ATTRIBUTES N º 2
Descriptive
Substance
Structure
Color
Form
Texture
Sound
Flavor
Smell
Space
Density

Of process
Marketing

Manufacture
Sale
Function
Time

Social
Responsibilities
Politics
Taboos

Of price
Cost of the manufacturer
Cost of the wholesaler
Cost of the perfectionist
Cost of the consumer

Morphologic analysis

This technique (also so called "Morphologic box") is one of the most valuable techniques to generate great quantity of ideas in a brief period of time. The astronomer Fritz Zwicky developed it based on technological works related to astrophysics and space investigations.

It is basically a combinatorial technique consistent in separating into its core elements (breaking down) a problem in its essential elements or basic parts. With its features or attributes we construct a table that allows us multiply the relations between these parts. This way, in its most basic form, Morphologic Analysis is nothing more than the generation of ideas by means of a table.

Therefore, this technique starts with a list of attributes to generate new possibilities.

The steps of the process are the following ones:

- Pick the problem to resolve, the situation or object to improve, etc.
- Analyze what attributes (elements or parameters) compose the problem. The attributes can refer to physical parts, to processes, to functions, to aesthetic aspects, etc. Here it is suitable to select the relevant attributes. Michalko proposes the convenience of formulating the following question to determine if an attribute is rele-

vant or not: "without this attribute, the problem would continue existing?".

- Analyze the variants or possible alternatives of every attribute.
- Combine all the possible combinations, picking every time a variant of each attribute (the total number of possible combinations is named a "morphologic product"). In other words, when the table is finished, it is about traveling through all the parameters and variations, selecting one or more from each column and, later on, combining them in completely new forms.

It can be carried out in two ways:

At random: choosing at random a variant of every attribute.

Enumeration: enumerating all the possible combinations, for later on, analyze them systematically. If the number of variants is high, the number of different combinations can become unmanageable. A usual simplification consists of eliminating those partial combinations of two or more variants that are considered to be unfit and, in consequence, of eliminating all of those that would stem from them.

Example:

A publisher is looking for new products and decides to work with four parameters: kinds of books, properties of the books, processes of edition and forms of information.

Table of ideas for a publishing house

	Class	Properties	Processes	Form
1	Fiction	Sound (Audio, books)	Acquisition of originals	Gift books in large format
2	Non fiction	Color	Production	Bulletin
3	Classic	Texture	Marketing	Anthologies
4	Books "how to..." (cook, sew, etc .)	Social Responsibilities	traditional or non traditional distribution	Software
5	Business	Illustrations	Writing software	Binding
6	Textbooks	Essence: paper or floppy disk	Discount	Rustic
7	Infantile	Smell	Advertising	Reward
8	Religion	Exercises, games or puzzle	Timeline from manuscript to finished product	Magazine
9	Mystery	Flavor	Knowledge or entertainment	free sheets
10	Sports	big, small or strange structure	Design and format	Bundled with other products

(From Michael Mihalko's "Thinkertoys")

As you will have noticed, the technique of Morphologic Analysis is quite adapted for generating ideas in an exploratory stage. But also let's not disdain its because of its complexity, especially when there are many combinations to produce.

We use this technique for new products or services (or modifications to some already existing ones), for applications to new materials, for looking for new marketing segments or for new ways of developing a competitive edge, for imagining new promotional techniques for products and services, etc.

CREATIVE COLLAGE [21]

Who hasn't cut and pasted a text found in Internet and later included it in a report or an article? Practically we all did this in some occasion.

If we ponder a while, cutting and pasting has a lot to do with the creation process. After all, we are providing a new solution with existing materials. On the other hand, repeating the ancient materials is no creation, it's just production.

Creative collage is one of the techniques of creativity.

The essence: to foment the free association of ideas and to promote creative thinking.

---

21   Many people show surprise when they realize that many of the creative techniques use senses and approaches that we don't commonly use. And that's true; most of those techniques appeal to the creation of psychologist states that will trigger our inner creativity. Creative collage is one of them.

Paradox

The paradox is an apparently contradictory affirmation.

Paradoxes are based on the meaning of the words, on their relation to reality and not only in their form. Formulating paradoxes forces us, therefore, to strain for discovering a vision different from the reality (critical or candid) and to re-formulate in an innocent way the contradictions that we observe.

The paradox needs attention, critical spirit, and endowments of observation and capacity of formulation.

Serves as an example of paradox this Yogi Berra's magnificent quotation: "Nobody goes there anymore because there are already too many people".

Playing with words allows us establish many creative reflexes.

Random words

It is the simplest of all the creative techniques. On the other hand it is very powerful, although this sounds quite illogical.

As soon as we have perfectly delimited the creative area on which we need the contribution of new ideas we pick a word that does not have any connection with the situation.

For example, looking for ideas on the problem of addictions we extract at random from the dictionary the word "semaphore":

Addictions = semaphore

From this juxtaposition we try to elaborate novel ideas.

The base of this technique is to force the brain to establish the necessary connections although the word that is obtained at random seems to be, initially, very remote from our problem.

The steps

Once looking for a new approach to a problem, pick a word at random (extracting it from the dictionary, from a newspaper, choosing it from a list or with any other method). It is transcendent to stick to the first word that pops up.

Think about a set of things (the more the better) that are associated with the selected word. This will force the connections with our creative area.

Later, elaborate a list of the ideas that have arisen.

List of random words

Bank	toe	toast	Insect
Tunnel	seed	soup	pink
Football	weed	hair dye	fly
Householder	bruise	beer	fossil
Bridge	washbasin	dipper	woman
Pulley	magnet	ploughed	shirt
Rope	spaghetti	mattress	pocket
It sweeps	I dial	setting Sun	pipe
On	thumbtack	door	rubber
Broadcast	cashier	cupboard	tie
Torpedo	bag	sink	bifocals
Knot	chain	television	gelatin
Fishhook	prison	shoe	egg
Meat	parasol	nut	branch
Cup	butter	bird	sword
Clock	cancer	stains	door
Eruption	plane	wedding ring	motive
Car	pill	came	monster
Travel	bill	taxes	museum
Zoo	tool	hook	fit
Chewing gum	moustache	chimney	tea
Razor	squirrel	poker	dropper
Barbecue	clown	gyratory	calls
Every	fireworks	language	fruit
Pits	cheese	tomato	fractures

PO

It is about an element that can be used in the creative phase of whatever technique we use.

PO is a word invented by De Bono. It can be understood as Provoking Operation's initials. Though, rather, it is a symbol and serves as a basic tool for lateral thinking.

It is used for giving "permission" to the people for exposing a hypothesis in order to explore it, not to evaluate it.

"Po" derives of "postulating". It is an invitation to escape from a concrete point of view in terms of good or bad and to use lateral thinking to go beyond that point of view.

Provocation is, in a certain way, a mental experiment. Many new ideas arise at random, by accident or by mistake. These facts produce a discontinuity that forces us to go beyond the habitual limits of what is "reasonable", that is established by our experience. The deliberate provocation is a systematical method that can produce the same effects.

Two are the basic uses of PO: to create provisional sets of information and to consider them to be sets of information provisionally established.

Forced relations

This technique consists of relating our problem or creative challenge to characteristics arisen from concepts or elements randomly picked, looking for new ideas that allow us develop original solutions.

The motive? Breaking down the perception frame an extending the creative horizon through relating concepts that do not have, at first, any apparent connection.

The first step for the utilization of this technique consists of picking a word that represents our problem.

Once the above-mentioned word is selected, we have to create a table with three columns. The header of the left column is "Concepts and elements stimuli" and its content will be those stimuli-words chosen at random. We will name the central column "Characteristics". There we will jot down the qualities of the concepts of the previous column. Finally, in the right column, we will put the new ideas arisen immediately after relating the previous characteristics to our problem or creative challenge.

Concepts and elements stimulus	Characteristics	New design

Once the table prepared, the methodology is:

1. Complete the column of stimuli with things picked at random. It is possible to as many words as you wish. Nevertheless, we recommend selecting at least five words, to obtain a suitable number of ideas.
2. Enunciate the qualities or the features typical of every stimulus. In this case we will have to find descriptions that are not only words, but also representative phrases.
3. Complete the column of ideas with associations or connections, taking each of the characteristics separately and relating them to the key word (the word that represents our problem).
4. Finally, it is about picking the ideas that look the most interesting or promising and try to improve them.

As an example, we develop here a table which principal topic is "kicking-off of a new shampoo".

Concepts and elements stimulus	Characteristics	New design
Instant coffee	- granulated	- Powder shampoo
	- mixed with water	- Shampoo that is prepared mixing it with a liquid
	- it is possible to prepare it weaker or stronger, depending on the quantity we put.	- for children or frequent use, we dilute it more

This technique stimulates originality because it allows us obtain distinctive characteristics or differentiated products. Hence it is especially useful for the creation of new products or services and for the creation of new lines of the same product.

4 x 4 x 4

It is a group technique where the assembled people produce ideas, first individually and, then in-group.

The technique achieves a notable quantitative production of ideas and, in parallel, increases the cohesion and the communication in the group.

To practice it, each participant individually writes down on a paper sheet four essential ideas about the creative topic (For example, "ideas for improving the efficiency of meetings").

Once finished this stage, the group forms in couples. Every couple seeks to come to an agreement and writes four essential ideas about the creative topic.

Later, they form groups of four people, and then eight and this way successively until the entire group has to reach an agreement and decide which are the four essential ideas about the creative topic or about the problem.

Four final ideas are the final qualitative result of the whole previous production.

It is fundamental, in this technique, that a facilitator is designated, as he will be the one who has to set the pace. He will interrupt every 6 to 10 minutes depending on the experience of the participants and on the existing cohesion in the group.

3

CREATIVE CHALLENGES

More important than the answer, the interesting thing is our mental process when we facing these challenges, so do not take this as a competition (we have already seen that this can hamper creativity)

How would you calculate the weight of a plane without using a scale?

~

How would you design Bill Gates' bath? [22]

~

You have eight pool balls. One of them has a flaw: it weighs less than the rest. To decide which one it is you have a scale that you can use only two times.

~

You have five jars full of pills. One of the jars contains defective pills. The only thing that differentiates them is that the good ones weigh 10 grams and the defective ones 9 grams.

You have a scale that you can use only once.

22   These are questions often asked in candidates' selection processes in several companies, where they want to probe into the creativity capacity through the solving of problems in both a creative and efficient way.

~

You pay one of your employees with a golden ounce a day. You have a golden rod which value is equivalent to his weekly wages. The bar is fragmented in seven equal parts but you can only make two cuts to it.

~

Find twenty-five different ways of dividing a square in four equal parts.

~

Michael and Maria have 21Euros between the two of them. Michael has 20 Euros more than Maria. How many Euros have each one of them?

~

Find at least 50 ways of defining the following figure:

Example: It forms of L, a set square, a reversed gallows, two rectangles, a right angle, half a frame of a picture, a big rectangle and a small one, etc.

~

Imagine that you have an apple pie. Cut it in eight slices doing only three cuts.

Notices that there are three alternatives as a minimum

~

Through mathematical operations where only can intervene nines, you have to obtain the number of 100 as the final result.

~

You are in a tennis court and prepare to collect all the balls littering the ground. You can choose between boxes with a capacity for two, three, four or five balls. In the moment of collecting the balls, if you use the boxes of two, one ball remains. If you pick the boxes of three, two balls remain. In those of four, three. And in those of five, four.

How many balls are there on the court?

~

How many telephone booths are there in your city?

~

In a nearby reservoir there are two fishes. On the following day four. And the following one, eight. And this way until the reservoir is overflowing with fish.
Which day were the fishes occupying half of the capacity of the reservoir?

~

How many gallons of paint are necessary to paint all the ships in the world?

~

A type of clock marks the hours with the most unimaginable precision, though it does only two times every day.

What clocks are we talking about?

~

Why are manholes round?

~

Of all the names in the list there is one that should not be in the list, provided that it does not match the common criteria, which is?

Ingrid
Victoria
Ricardo
Xavier
Lorraine
Carlos
David
Daisy

~

Transform the EDC series into many series simultaneously with a single change of letter

~

If the barber shaves only those people who do not shave themselves, then who shaves the barber?

~

You think in front of a closed door that opens onto a room. The room is in the dark. In it there is a bulb, but from where you are you cannot see if it is on or off.

Where you are there are four switches of which only one ignites the bulb in the room of the other side.

You can activate or deactivate the switches all the times you want, but you can enter the room only once.

How would you do decide which is the switch that sets the bulb up?

~

You are at a famous international golf tournament and this top competitor had a great possibility of winning it.

His blow with an "iron" had landed at a scanty distance from the "green", which was giving it a good opportunity to annotate with a blow under par.

With a wide smile he walked along the "fairway" and stopped with a gesture of disappointment.

The ball had rolled inside a small paper bag that some of the spectators had dropped littering the ground. If he decided to take the ball out of the bag, this would count as an additional strike. If he decides to strike the bag and the ball, he would lose the control of the shot.

What should he do?

~

The moths use to gnaw at the books page after page and by doing so plow ahead across the volumes.

One of those insects, gnawing, drilled its way from the first page of the first volume of a book up to the last one of the second volume, which was next to the first one.

Every volume has 800 pages. How many pages did the moth gnaw at?

~

Lucy was born on a sunny Sunday in Hong Kong and made seven in a gray and rainy Sunday in Macao.

How old was she in 1996?

~

A young man seriously wounded in a car accident is driven to urgencies at the hospital. The doctor diagnoses that it is necessary to carry out brain surgery ASAP.

Therefore the presence of a doctor specialist in brain surgery is requested. The doctor after seeing the patient exclaims: "I cannot operate this boy! He is my son!"

Nevertheless, the surgeon is not the biological father of the young man.

How do you explain this apparent contradiction?

~

What is the million dollars question?

~

Why are bullrings round?

~

What's the taste of happiness?

~

Divide this area into four equal parts, so each of them contains the numbers from 1 to 4.

3	2	1	1
3	1	4	3
4	3	2	4
2	2	1	4

You have 15 seconds to count all the F letters in the following text.

You have a piece of paper (A4) and a pair of scissors. The challenge is to achieve that two people get together across that piece of paper.
The only available resources are the piece of paper and the scissors. Nothing more, except yourselves...
You can manipulate and cut the paper but the page must remain in a single piece.

Two women play checkers. They play 5 games with no draw and each woman wins the same number of games. How is this possible?

A child goes to bed, feeling very tired, at 7 p.m. The child has a lesson of piano and he sets the alarm of the clock for 8:45. How long will the child sleep?

⁓

On a table there was a basket with 6 apples and 6 girls in the room. Every girl took an apple and, nevertheless, an apple stayed in the basket. How could that be?

⁓

You are tired of receiving spam e-mail (propaganda, chains etc.) and you are looking for a solution. Your random word is BANANA.
You need to tell a tale to your son before going to bed. Your random word is EGG.

⁓

Unfortunately we have just lost our job. Nevertheless, we have just had an encouraging interview and probably an opportunity exists. The boss, the guy whom I have met, is an old-fashioned obnoxious guy. He has an archaic system to control his collaborators, although it works.
The boss can leave his office through any of the four doors of his office and, actually, he wants to see all his people busy. He told us that he is not ready to sack any of his current collaborators.
We will get a job at this company if we place ourselves in a spot where, when the boss steps out (through any of the 4 doors), he always sees 9 people working (nine exactly). Obviously, placing ourselves in the boss office is not the solution to this challenge.

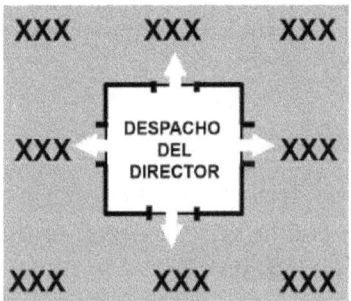

~

Take a piece of paper and a pen. You have only 60 seconds to write the largest number of white and edible things.

~

Take a piece of paper. Jot down the largest possible number of absolutely impossible situations.

~

How many squares can be obtained from the following figure?

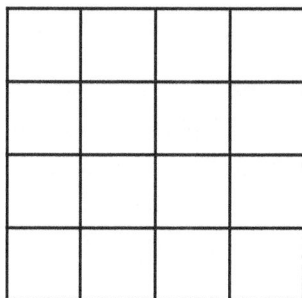

~

Pick at random an object that you've got close at hand. Then enumerate in 60 seconds all its possible uses.

~

Take a piece of paper. Annotate the greatest number of round, red and not edible objects.

~

Join nine dots with four right lines without raising the pen from the paper and without passing twice for the same point. If you achieve it, then try - with the same rules - to join now nine dots with three straight lines.

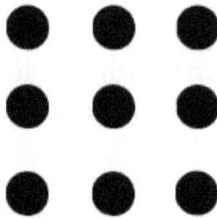

Enumerate all the ways you can think of about how to use a newspaper.

It is midnight in a big city. In one of the flats of an enormous building lives a doctor. The telephone rings. The wife of the doctor hears it and gets up to answer it. The caller is a woman. She asks for the doctor. The woman wakes her husband up and he asks, "Who is this?", the person on the line hangs up the telephone.

Who was the caller and why did the caller hang up?

In the attached drawing there are several tennis balls. The challenge is to divide the field in 5 sections so that every section contains 3 balls. You can use only three straight lines to split the field.

~

Take the dictionary and pick four words at random. Based on some criterion, identify the word that does not fit. Explain the criterion.
(Avoid the most obvious reasons such as the same number of letters, etc.)

~

Take a piece of paper and a pair of scissors. Draw a figure like the one that appears down below and, then, with a single cut produce the figure. It is allowed to realize only a cut with the scissors and it has to be a straight cut.

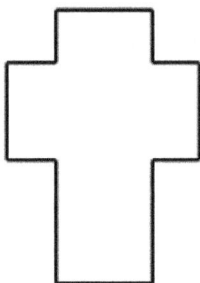

~

You have 60 seconds to enumerate all the round and blue things that come to your mind.

~

Enumerate all the ways of using a brick.

~

Take a newspaper or a magazine and pick four words at random. Then create a history using the chosen words.

~

How can you define a bottle of milk of a liter that contains half a liter of water?

~

You have six matches. The challenge consists of forming four triangles with them without crossing of breaking the matches.

~

Look for five new arguments to convince your teenager son not to spend so much time playing at the computer.

~

You have one minute to make a list of forty words that begin with the letter "P"?

~

Turn the Roman number IX into six adding only one line.

IX

~

A twenty-eight-year-old man had to walk during twenty-five minutes under a strong downpour. He was not wearing any hat, had neither an umbrella nor any element to cover himself. Nevertheless, he was not soaked.
Give an explanation to this surprising feat.

~

Without looking at your wristwatch, make a drawing of it as exactly as possible. Later, compare your drawing to the watch.

~

Write on a piece of paper ten words that define you as a person or as professional. Later, bearing this information in mind, draw an emblem that represents you.

Imagine that in this equation each of the small sticks it is a match. Please modify the equation (it is incorrect!) without touching the matches, without adding new matches or without eliminating any of them.

$$XI + I = X$$

~

Pick the word FLAVOUR. Combine its letters in any ways. How many words do you obtain? How many of them do make sense? Then invent a definition for those that don't have any meaning at all.

~

Write a list, as long as possible, of things that make noise.

~

Two friends, Albert and Jimmy, who had not met for many years casually meet in the street. In a moment of the conversation Albert asks Jimmy: "How old are your daughters?". "The product of their ages is 36 - answers Jimmy - and the sum happens to be the number of your house". After thinking a bit, Albert exclaims: "I lack some information". "It is true", affirms Jimmy, "I had forgotten to tell you that the elder plays piano".

How old are Jimmy's daughters?

~

What's the taste of the color green? (Explain the meaning and the reason of the response)

~

Write the number 100 with only four 9.

~

You are in a room with a marble floor. How do you drop an egg from one-meter height without breaking the shell?

~

A person agonizes in the hospital victim of an assault. The police brings before the moribund three suspects: Díaz, Martínez and Perez. The victim cannot move and can barely emit audible sounds, but he manages to say, without indicating anybody: "He was the assassin". All in the room conclude that it was Díaz. Why?

~

A landowner says to his gardener: "Here you have ten trees. Plant them in the garden so that they form five rows of four trees each one". Can you help the gardener?

~

Expresses each of the first ten numbers with four "fours".

~

Describes a spiral staircase without doing any spiraling gesture with your hand.

~

Mention twenty-five objects that have a square.

~

Take a piece of paper and make the most possible number of noises with it.

~

A man lies in a field. At his side there is an unopened package. There is nobody else in the field. A passerby approaches the place where the lying man rests, and he immediately knows that the man is whether already dead or bound to die soon. How does he know it? How did he die?

~

A lady forgot her driving license at home. She jumped a rail pass, neglected a one-way signal and then traveled three blocks the wrong way.

~

A traffic cop, who, nevertheless, did not make any attempt to stop her, observed the entire scene. Why?

~

Uria Fuller, famous for its psychic prowess, is capable of revealing the scoreboard of a football match before it has even begun. So far he has never failed.
How is it possible that he always succeeds?

~

We have two tins full of water and a large empty container. Is there any way of putting all of the water inside the big container so we can distinguish which water came out from every tin?

~

4

FINAL STEP: PERSONAL CREATIVITY PROGRAM

Hereafter are included a series of ideas that will help you develop your creativity. The program is designed in order that, once you finish it, you will start enjoying the refreshing effects of being a creative person.

The ideas we suggest arise from ideas that participants have shared with us during our creativity sessions; from things we have read about or listened to, or, simply, from personal occurrences.

Do you accept the challenge and start with the program?

Personal program (day 1)

Create a "stock of smiles". Collect things that make you laugh or simply think more. Cut articles from magazines, cartoons or ads that thrill you and stock them together so you'll be able to obtain instantaneous inspiration when you need it.

Personal program (day 2)

Play during 10 minutes to "What would happen if...". The goal of this game is to think about strange situations. "What would happen if paper was illegal?" The more ridiculous it is the better. Record a minimal number of ideas.

Personal program (day 3)

Buy or borrow three magazines that you would normally not read. Then consider the following questions: How does every magazine approach the different topics? How do they connect with their readers? What does each of them do in a different way?

Personal program (day 4)

Make a list of concrete things that you can do to clear your mind. Try hard, so the list contains at least 15 different ideas. Once the list is made, keep it always at hand and consult it when you face mental blockades.

Personal program (day 5)

Today it is Saturday. Go outdoors: drive, walk, run, and mount on bicycle. Go to some new place and then explore the surroundings. Focus on everything you see.

Personal program (day 6)

Take a long bath. You will be surprised at the number of ideas that come to your mind.

Personal program (day 7)

Create different topics for each day of the week, as routine from Monday until Friday can affect creativity. So celebrate every day with a different motto, like for instance "Friday: gastronomy day" or "Monday: movies day".

Important: it must be something that you are not currently doing.

PERSONAL PROGRAM (DAY 8)

Today it is the day of "zero remorse". Try something new, do something unfamiliar to you. The only rule is: do not hesitate or repent of what you do in the whole day.

PERSONAL PROGRAM (DAY 9)

Learn three new things about the people you are working with today. Ask them about their lives. How many brothers or sisters do they have? What is their favorite recollection of childhood? If they were a superhero, which one would they be?

PERSONAL PROGRAM (DAY 10)

Create a story with 5 people with whom you are today. You can include from the person at your side when buying the newspaper up to the people who has attended you when you have gone to the supermarket.

PERSONAL PROGRAM (DAY 11)

Today book 15 minutes and start writing compulsively. Write everything that comes to your mind. Without any exception. If you can't think of anything at all, just write that you can't think of anything at all. No idea or concept is bad. Do not judge, do not analyze, do not stop writing everything what passes through your head until the end of the 15 minutes.

PERSONAL PROGRAM (DAY 12)

Annotate all the forms, sounds, colors and textures that you perceive in the room where you currently are.

PERSONAL PROGRAM (DAY 13)

Today it is Saturday. Go to your kitchen. Look what's in the fridge. Have a glimpse at what you have in the pantry. Try to cook a dish that you have never cooked before with the products that you have at hand. Beware! Do not prepare what you have seen other people cook or what you have already prepared in the past.

PERSONAL PROGRAM (DAY 14)

At some moment today, sing a song aloud.

PERSONAL PROGRAM (DAY 15)

Take a piece of paper and start writing a story (on the most peculiar topic, as for example "The flying pencil"). When you have written the first line, hand the paper to the person next to you. Ask him to add a new line before handing it over to another person. The more participants, the better. At the end of the week, gather all the written material and read the final story aloud.

PERSONAL PROGRAM (DAY 16)

Devote 5 minutes to complete an exercise of free association. In the center of a paper sheet write a word. During the above-mentioned time, write everything what comes to your mind in relation to this word, creating ramifications from it. "Restaurant" can take you to "greasy food" and from there to "heart failure" and from there to "falling in love". When time is over, check everything that you have written. Can you see new connections that you had not contemplated before?

Personal program (day 17)

Throughout this week, when you are going to make a comment or when your opinion is asked, always begin with a positive phrase.

(With this exercise you will be able to modify your way of seeing things and avoiding the human trend for considering always the negative part of things).

Personal program (day 18)

Look around you. Focus your attention on an object at random in your visual field at this moment. Strain for finding, as minimum, ten different uses for the object in question.

Personal program (day 19)

When walking in the street, concentrate on a person at random. Use creativity to invent his possible life.

Personal program (day 20)

Open a dictionary and pick at random five adjectives or five nouns. Invent a history that relates those words. Write the history down. Read it and then enrich the history with details or new developments.

Personal program (day 21)

Buy yourself a notebook and annotate some quotations you like. They can be from famous authors, from movies, from newspapers....

Anytime you face a problem, select one of the quotations and relate it to the problem.

Personal program (day 22)

Pick a familiar object and use your five senses. Once you have finished, think about what it has suggested to you.

When facing a problem, value it in this same way. What do you feel when analyzing it? What sound does it bring to your memory? What smell, flavor or sensation does it remind you of while thinking about it?

Personal program (day 23)

Re-design your office. If you do not have office, then re-design the room where you spend the most time in the day.

Paint it a different color, change some furniture, switch the places of things, hang up new photographies, put a new screensaver, modify the orientation of the table, etc.

Personal program (day 24)

Today it is the day for flexibility, the day for freeing ourselves from our habits.

Today just modify your habits as soon as you get up (hour, breakfast, routine...). Change the transportation way with which you go to work. Throughout today change your way of answering the phone.

5

BIBLIOGRAPHY

Bacus, Anne and Roman, C. Creativity. How to develop it. Editorial Iberia. Barcelona. 1994.

Blackmore, Susan The machine of the memes. Editorial Paidós. Barcelona. 2000.

Boden, Margaret A. The creative mind. Myths and mechanisms. Editorial Gedisa. Barcelona. 1994.

Buzán, T. The book of the mental maps. Editions Uranus. Madrid. 1996.

Buzán, T. How to create mental maps. Editions Uranus. Madrid. 2002.

Clegg, B. and Birch, P. Creativity to the instant. Editions Granica. 2001.

Corrals, J. The creative management. Publishing Auditorium. Madrid. 1991.

Csikszentmihalyi, M. Creativity. Editorial Paidós Ibérica. Barcelona. 1998.

Csikszentmihalyi, M. (Flow) flows. Editorial Kairós. Barcelona. 2007.

De Bono. You design for professionals who think. Editorial Paidós. Barcelona. 1991.

De Bono. The lateral Thinking. Manual of creativity. Editorial Paidós. Barcelona. 1986.

De Bono. Six hats to think. Paidós Ibérica. Barcelona. 2008.

De Bono. Creativity. 62 exercises to develop the mind. Paidós Ibérica. Barcelona. 2008.

Of the Tower, Saturnine. Applied creativity. Resources for a creative training. Publishing Teaching of the River Plate. Buenos Aires. 2007.

Of the Tower, Saturnine and Violant, Verónica. To understand and to evaluate creativity. Editions Cistern. Malaga. 2006.

Demory, B. Techniques of creativity. Granica. Barcelona. 1997.

Epstein, R. The great book of the games of creativity. Activities rapid and entertaining to stimulate the inventiveness. Oniro. Barcelona. 2002.

Foster, T.R. 101 methods to generate ideas. How to stimulate creativity. Editions Deusto. Barcelona. 2002.

Galician, F. To learn to generate ideas: to innovate by means of creativity. Editions Paidós Ibérica. Barcelona. 2002.

Gardner, H. Creative minds. An anatomy of creativity. Paidós. Barcelona. 1995.

Hogarth, R. M. To educate the intuition. The development of the sixth sense. Paidós. Barcelona. 2002.

Kriegel, R. J. and Patler, L. If it is not broken break it. Not conventional ideas for a business changeable world. Editions Management 2000. Barcelona. 2001.

Lamata, R. The creative attitude. Exercises to be employed at group creativity. Editions Narcea. Madrid. 2005.

Marín, Ricardo and De la Torre, Saturnine. Manual of creativity. Educational applications. Publishing Vicens Vives. Barcelona. 2000.

Sea-coast, J. A. Theory of the creative intelligence. Publishing Anagram. Barcelona. 1993.

Maslow, A. The creative Personality. Kairós. Barcelona. 7 ª ed. 2001.

Medina, To. You design to have ideas. How to be creative without having a pinch of imagination. Pearson Education. Madrid. 2007.

Menchén, F. To discover creativity. Editions Pyramid. Madrid. 2001.

Michalko, M. The secrets of the geniuses of creativity. (Cracking creativity). Editions Management 2000. Barcelona. 2000.

Michalko, M. Thinker toys. How to develop creativity in the company. Editions Management 2000. Barcelona. 2001.

Muñoz Adánez, To. Creative methods for organizations. Editions Pyramid. Barcelona. 2006.

Ponti, F. The creative company. Granica. EADA Direction Barcelona. 2001.

Ponti, F. and Ferràs, X. Passion for innovating. From the idea to the result. Granica. Barcelona. 2006.

Bridge Ferreras, To. The creative brain. Publishing alliance. Madrid. 1999.

Renart, J. B. Creativity applied to the company. Editions Management 2000. Barcelona. 2003.

Rodari, G. Grammar of the fantasy. Introduction to the art of inventing histories. Editions of the Bronze. Barcelona. 1996.

Rodríguez, M. Manual of creativity. Publishing Threshings. Mexico. 1995.

Rodríguez, M. The creative integral thinking. Publishing Mc Graw-Hill. Mexico. 1997.

Roman J.D. The paper bridge. LER. Buenos Aires. 2006.

Blunt, Manuela. Psychology of creativity. Paidós. Barcelona. 1997.

Sternberg, R. J. and Lubart, T. I. Creativity in a culture conformist. A challenge to the masses. Publishing Paidós Ibérica. Barcelona. 1997.

Zelinski, E. J. To think to the big thing. Exercises simple and entertained to promote creativity. Editions Oniro. Barcelona. 2001.

ÍNDICE

Prologue

LibrosEnRed Publishing House

LibrosEnRed is the most complete digital publishing house in the Spanish language. Since June 2000 we have published and sold digital and printed-on-demand books.

Our mission is to help all authors publish their work and offer the readers fast and economic access to all types of books.

We publish novels, stories, poems, research theses, manuals, and monographs. We cover a wide range of contents. We offer the possibility to commercialize and promote new titles through the Internet to millions of potential readers.

Our royalties system allows authors to receive a profit 300% to 400% greater than they would obtain in the traditional circuit.

Enter www.librosenred.com to see our catalog, comprising of hundreds of classic titles and contemporary authors.

www.ingramcontent.com/pod-product-compliance
Lightning Source LLC
Chambersburg PA
CBHW020705270326
41928CB00005B/269